Catechizing For Justice

A Six-Session Program To Promote The Gospel Mission

Janet I. Miller

B261-3

Resource Publications, Inc.
San Jose, California

To my mother, Phyllis Matteis,
my primary catechist who nurtured me
in the ways of justice.

Reprint Department
Resource Publications, Inc.
160 E. Virginia Street #290
San Jose, CA 95112-5876
1-408-286-8505 voice
1-408-287-8748 fax

ISBN 0-89390-516-X

Printed in the United States of America

01 02 03 04 05 | 5 4 3 2 1

Editorial director: Nick Wagner
Production artists: Mike Sagara, Nelson Estarija
Copyeditor: Laura Quilling

Contents

Preface

*I*n the 1980s I took a course titled "Peace and Justice" as part of my studies for a master's degree in catechetics in Santa Clara University's Pastoral Ministries Program. I was captivated by the richness of our social tradition and by how the Catholic Church has developed the teachings of God's just reign. I was disturbed, however, to realize that as the church, we have a social teaching treasury of papal encyclicals and bishops' statements that remain unread and unheard of by so many of the faithful. I asked myself how, as a catechist for all my adult life, I had never heard of anyone using these teachings in any significant way.

Upon graduation, I became part of the master catechist formation team for the Diocese of Fresno and Rite of Christian Initiation of Adults director at St. Joseph parish in Firebaugh, California. To me, spreading the message of social justice became imperative. With the assistance of team members, I began to work on ways to incorporate justice awareness into our catechetical processes. The sessions in this book have emerged from that experience.

Since that time, numerous Catholic writers have sought to make our best kept secret, Catholic social teaching, known. Our bishops have, indeed, declared that teaching on the social mission be integrated into all catechesis. This renewed awareness has brought a great need for justice catechetical materials to help parishes and dioceses present the mission message. My hope is that *Catechizing for Justice* will make church social teaching a reality for an ever-growing number of faithful. When we all help each other envision the mission, Christ's redeeming work of love and justice will be lived throughout the world.

Acknowledgments

I am indebted to the Pastoral Ministries Program at Santa Clara University. I am especially thankful to Anne Marie Mongoven, OP, who inspired the vision for this justice catechesis; to Steve Privett, SJ, who brought me to awareness of the imperative of justice; and to Rita Claire Dorner, OP, who helped me understand the meaning of breaking ourselves open for others.

I thank all the people of the Diocese of Fresno who have journeyed with me in faith formation. I cannot recount all the suggestions that helped hone these sessions. I especially thank Teresa Dominguez for reading and critiquing the work in progress. I also thank Wanda Scheuermann at Resource Publications, Inc., for helping me polish the text. I express my gratitude to all who have decided to provide this catechesis in parishes so that more of the faithful will take ownership of the justice mission and will strive to make God's just reign a lived reality for all.

Introduction

*T*his resource is offered in response to the U.S. bishops' request "to incorporate the principles of Catholic social teaching into all materials and disciplines in addition to providing resources specific to Catholic social thought" ("Sharing Catholic Social Teaching" 105). This justice catechesis offers six sessions for believers to explore the social teachings of the church in an integrated fashion. Each session is designed to acquaint the participants with aspects of justice by drawing on Scripture and ecclesial social documents. The purpose of the program is more than informational, however. The sessions offer opportunities for prayer, reflection, and mutual support so that, as participants experience their own deeper calls to conversion, they are nurtured by each other and the Spirit. Throughout the sessions, members will have opportunities to grapple with the major justice themes and will be challenged to integrate the social mission with their life decisions. In the justice catechetical process, believers are encouraged to connect these themes with their own experiences as well as with the experience of the greater society so that they may see new ways of living for the common good.

The catechesis will familiarize members with pieces of papal and episcopal documents so that believers will develop ownership of the social teaching. The benefits of this approach are twofold: First, the participants can gain insight that justice action is not for only a fringe element but is an integral way of living for believers as explained and developed in the social teaching documents. Second, members may be inspired to read these documents themselves to benefit even more fully from the richness of the church's justice tradition.

These catechetical sessions are designed for a wide variety of catechetical needs. The series may be offered
- as a Lenten renewal program in a parish;
- as a mystagogy or postbaptismal catechesis for the neophytes;
- for teacher and catechist formation;
- as a continuation of RENEW or small community sharing groups;
- as a unit in ministry formation programs;
- for general ongoing adult catechesis;
- or with adaptations for older youth so they can draw on church teaching in making choices and finding a life path.

Using This Book

This book provides a complete catechetical process to introduce believers to the social teaching and thereby to call them to live according to the church mission. "Preparing for the Process" (below) gives extensive information and suggestions for planning the program. The six sessions are completely outlined and include preparation guides and reproducible background notes and handouts. An evaluation tool is provided to use after the sessions for further planning. The resource appendix has suggestions for making a parish profile and a myriad of supplemental resources and reference ideas.

The seven major themes of Catholic social teaching are explored in six catechetical sessions. These principles are presented in an integrated fashion.

The goal is to help participants integrate the social mission of the church with their daily decisions and activities. Each session begins with a welcome, a prayer, and a section that links our own human experience to an area of social justice. Then the members reflect on Scripture and church teaching in light of current social conditions. During refreshment time, the group has an opportunity to bond more deeply. After the break the members share insights gained during the time together and consider how they are being called to live more justly. Each session concludes with a prayer experience designed to send them forth to live the social mission of the church more fully.

Preparing for the Process

The pastor or parish director may recruit catechists or leaders for the sessions. One person may be the facilitator for all six sessions, or the responsibilities may be shared by a team. Before planning the process, the leader or team is encouraged to read the background notes and sessions, meditate on suggested Scripture, and read the reference passages in the documents. (See the document list under "Materials.")

Invitations to participate in this justice catechesis may be offered in the parish bulletin, on bulletin boards, through the parish phone tree or e-mail system, and by other means of communication. People will feel invited to attend when registration forms are readily available with easy-to-return instructions. For planning purposes, preregistration is encouraged; however, in the spirit of justice, the invitation to join should remain for newcomers to feel welcome at any point.

Those organizing the sessions can refer to the "Materials" section to gather basic supplies needed for every session (for example, Bibles, pencils, paper, masking tape, name tags). These supplies can be placed in a special box. The preparation page for each session lists additional materials needed for that specific session. Copies of the handouts can be made ahead of time and placed in a portable file for easy access. Only the handouts and background notes (marked with the people emblem) may be reproduced by the purchaser of this book for use in these sessions.

Those who purchase this book are free to adapt the materials for their local needs. Because a parish profile is a useful tool in adapting catechesis, parish profile worksheets are included in the resource appendix for parishes that may not have a profile on file. The leader or team can use the data to tailor the process to the particular social justice concerns of the parish and to determine a starting point. The members' current understandings regarding church social teaching will determine the necessary approach. To select an emphasis, identify your parish from one or a combination of the following models. Is your parish one with

- little previous exposure to Catholic social teaching, needing basic vocabulary and introduction to the documents?
- some social ministries, but seeking to involve more members in outreach?
- an active outreach, but realizing the need for more prayer to integrate their efforts?
- an active outreach program, but realizing the need to ground the work in Catholic social teaching?

- the need to break a misconception that justice work is only for a radical few?
- the need to empower members to seek justice regarding their own socioeconomic condition?

Choose options and adaptations that will help the members and the entire parish grow according to their specific needs.

Catechizing for Justice Objectives

The following are the overall objectives of social justice awareness catechesis. This process

- encourages the participants to nurture and empower one another to live the Gospel message of justice.
- invites members to identify with people of other cultures.
- examines the ordered system of rights and responsibilities.
- reflects on situations of injustice.
- explores Scripture passages that relate to justice themes.
- acquaints believers with documents that delineate church social teaching.
- provides opportunities for discussion.
- strengthens the members' sense of community.
- joins the social mission to prayer.
- offers time to socialize.

Materials

The following is a list of materials that are generally needed for every session. Refer to the preparation page of each session for additional materials:

- a copy of "Preparation for Each Session Checklist" found at the end of this section
- name tags, newsprint, markers, Bibles, pens and/or pencils, paper, masking tape
- candle, cloth, seasonal sign, percussion instrument
- musician or tape/CD player, songbooks or words reproduced with permission
- coffee, tea, sugar, creamer, cups, napkins, other refreshments items

Obtaining Materials: In the spirit of justice, consider obtaining materials from sources that are known to foster human dignity. Work of Human Hands (800-685-7572) directly markets goods made by artisans from around the world. By purchasing articles from this source, believers help other people reach their potential and maintain their dignity as providers for themselves and their families. The use of these items in catechesis models just stewardship and solidarity.

Many of the items for prayer and some refreshments are available from this source. Check out their supply of candles, holders, baskets and other containers, cloths, and religious symbols. They have a variety of percussion instruments for the call to prayer or to offer members during singing. Choose from a variety of coffees and teas, and try to be creative with some of the food items they make available.

Documents for the Resource Center: I hope this justice catechesis will inspire members to read some of the church's rich social doctrine treasury. I strongly advise setting up a resource center with the major documents and other reference materials. Encourage members to check out the booklets. Suggest that beginners skim them for topics covered in the session instead of trying to read them cover to cover. Most documents are available in booklets from the United States Catholic Conference Publishing Services (800-235-8722). They offer great prices for members and quantity discounts. It is good to have one copy of *Catholic Social Thought: The Documentary Heritage* by O'Brien and Shannon for documents that may be out of print and to have a reference index; however, individual documents are easier to share and less intimidating to handle. See the resource appendix for additional information and possibilities. Try to have the following documents and books available:

Papal Documents
Rerum Novarum: On the Condition of Workers
Quadgragesimo Anno: After Forty Years
Mater et Magistra: Christianity and Social Progress
Pacem in Terris: Peace on Earth
Populorum Progressio: On the Development of Peoples
Octogesima Adveniens: A Call to Action: Apostolic Letter on the Eightieth
   Anniversary of Rerum Novarum
Evangelii Nuntiandi: On Evangelization in the Modern World
Sollicitudo Rei Socialis: On Social Concern
Centesimus Annus: On the Hundredth Anniversary of Rerum Novarum
Tertio Millennio Adveniente: On the Coming of the Third Millennium
Respect for Human Rights: The Secret of True Peace

From the Bishops
Justice in the World (1971)
Economic Justice for All

Compiled Church Teachings
The Documents of Vatican II (*Guadium et Spes* and *Lumen Gentium*)
Catechism of the Catholic Church

Sessions

Each session is planned in a two-hour format for a meeting once a week. The design allows for community-building social time and prayer for spiritual support. The time allotted to the human experience element is important for connecting theory and real life. In selecting session dates and times, seek to meet the needs of all members who may wish to attend. The following time schedule will help in planning and may be altered for group needs and specific sessions.

Opening: Welcome and Prayer	15 minutes
From Our Experience	20 minutes
Scripture and Tradition	40 minutes
Break	10 minutes
Called to Live Justly	25 minutes
Group Prayer	10 minutes

Meeting Space: Set up the meeting space so that all have a good view of one another and the presentation materials. Whenever possible, you should provide tables so that the members have a stable surface for writing and other items. When the tables are arranged in a U-shape with chairs on the outer sides, members are able to have eye contact for better communication with one another. For discussion in small groups, members may move chairs around the tables or into circles so they face one another. The leader may want to substitute a marker board or chalkboard, when available, for the newsprint suggested in the sessions. Note that before choosing a video option, planners should check out the condition and placement of VCR equipment.

The meeting space should be arranged to accommodate a separate prayer space. If desired, the prayer space may be in another area such as a vestibule, adjacent room, chapel, or outside in good weather. The procession to and from a prayer space sets off this time for communication with God.

Prayer Space: The focus of the prayer space may be a small table (or a counter area) covered with a liturgically appropriate colored cloth with space for the members to gather around. Colors for major liturgical seasons are violet during Lent and Advent, white during Easter and Christmas, and green for Ordinary Time. For extra richness, check a liturgical calendar and use red on a martyr's feast day and white on a memorial day, and include corresponding prayer intercessions. Open the Bible to a reading that will be used in the prayer, and add a candle with matches handy. Have a percussion instrument nearby to strike as a call to prayer.4

A liturgical and/or seasonal sign completes a prayerful environment. The seasonal sign reminds believers of God, who gives all gifts of creation. Flower arrangements, possibly picked by members from their home gardens, are a customary seasonal sign. During Lent a budding branch may be displayed; during Easter, Easter lilies. Rocks, shells, water, and other natural items are also appropriate. The liturgical sign is a reminder of the church year. Examples are a statue of a saint on a feast day, the rosary during the month of October, or an Advent wreath during December.

Using Music: Since St. Augustine gave us the tradition of singing as a way to "pray twice," the leader is encouraged to accommodate the prayer space for music. Ideally, a musician may lead the singing; however, a tape or CD player may be used. The leader will need to check for outlets, provide cords or batteries, and obtain the tapes or CDs. The songs need to be simple so all are encouraged to participate. With a hesitant group, substitute songs from parish liturgy, or encourage them to sing the refrain only. When making substitutions, choose music that awakens participation and reflects social themes.

The songs suggested in the sessions are from *A Eucharistic People* by Julie and Tim Smith and *A Remembering Heart* by Monica Brown. Both are available from Resource Publications, Inc., 160 E. Virginia St., Suite 290, San Jose, CA 95112 (408-286-8505). In the interest of justice, check with publishers before reproducing any words to selected songs.

Hints and Strategies

Hints for Effective Catechesis: Offer name tags at the beginning of each session so members can comfortably get to know one another. Reusable name tags can be made easily by attaching a three-foot piece of yarn to a three-inch square heavy card. Name tags not picked up at every session can be set aside as a quick way to keep track of attendance. The leader or other members may call those who are absent to sincerely inquire about health or other problems. Such follow-up gives the leader an opportunity to work with someone who may have become hesitant.

Set up a resource display table to help make the church social teaching more available to the members. In addition to the previously suggested encyclicals, provide other publications by the U.S. bishops, lists of websites, and materials from organizations that seek justice. Encourage members to check out materials and add a few new ones each week that relate to the theme. The background notes also may be reproduced for this purpose. Inexpensive prayer cards and bookmarks are available from Columban Fathers (402-291-1920). See the resource appendix for possibilities and contact information.

Use creative methods to break into small groups that respect human dignity so that no person feels left out. The leader directs small group assignments in a way that offers community building for all members with one another. Some simple ways to form small groups are to count off or form groups by first or last name initials. A fun method is to pass a basket of small colored candies, and those who get the same color form each group. The process should be quick and mix the group in different combinations at various times.

Remember that the proposed time schedule is only a planning guide. Since good catechesis emerges from the needs of the members, the plan often must be adjusted for questions and concerns. Respect the needs of all by beginning and ending on time. In adjusting the schedule, highlight the significance of prayer by allowing for a meaningful, unhurried experience. Go with the energy of the group, and be guided by the Spirit.

Strategies for Facilitating Justice Catechesis: Strategy hints for facilitating a social justice process are found in the preparation for each session. The leader may find it useful to look over all of these before the first session and draw on the hints as needed in the process. Discussion leaders need to address difficult justice topics in a positive manner that keeps hearers open and receptive. Justice demands a respect for the members' right to make their own choices and decisions.

Since church social teaching often touches delicate issues, leaders may identify areas of concern by referring to the parish profile and the registration forms. The leader may direct discussion away from these areas until the group members have had an opportunity to build a rapport with one another. During the process, hard issues certainly must be faced, and comfort zones will be stretched. The challenge for the leader is to direct the process in a gentle enough way to keep a nonthreatening environment.

As members gain interest in justice matters, they will need guidance to channel their reactions constructively. At first some may feel overwhelmed and helpless. Others may have an initial fervor to "cure it all." The leader can help them realize the first steps and how preparation precedes action.

Remember that prayer is vital to help members connect their own justice works to those of the church's mission. In subjugating our intentions to the will of the Creator and guidance of the Spirit, we join our justice efforts to Christ's redemptive work in the world. With our busy schedules, however, we sometimes are tempted to postpone prayer. The leader needs to pray before each session and provide special prayer time for the members. Those seeking justice are in need of the strengths and guidance of holy wisdom.

Because you picked up this book, you have identified yourself as one of the servants of the mission. Enjoy the process, and be inspired by the good people who will join you in this journey for justice. Empower others with the joy and hope that bring the peace of salvation to a turbulent world.

Catechesis Registration Form

Last name: _____

First name and middle initial:_____

Nickname:_____

Address: _____

Mailing address (if not the same): _____

Business address: _____

Phone number(s):

*day:*_____ *evening:* _____

cell:_____ *e-mail:* _____

Which contact number do you prefer?_____

Spouse's name, if applicable:_____

Children's names/ages:

_____

_____

_____

Your age range: < 20 years   21–35 years   36–69 years   > 70 years

Preferred language: _____

Days/times best for sessions:_____

Parish ministries in which you are involved: _____

_____

Other interests or additional comments: _____

_____

Preparation Checklist for Each Session

- Ahead of time, check that all materials for the particular session are available. Make any necessary phone calls.
- Read over the session, Scripture, and references to sections of documents.
- Choose options, and decide any adaptations.
- Arrange for a musician, or have CD or tapes and player.
- Obtain songbooks, or reproduce songs with permission.
- Make copies of handouts.
- Make coffee, and set the refreshment table.
- Set out special needs for the session (for example, videos, posters).
- Set chairs and tables in a U-shape. Have all materials handy to this area.
- Set a prayer table with liturgical colored cloth, Bible, candle, and seasonal sign.
- Take some time for personal prayer. Ask for guidance from the spirit of wisdom.
- List any special items or preparations for this session:

_____

_____

_____

_____

_____

_____

_____

_____

_____

_____

_____

The Sessions

Human Dignity and Human Rights

Background Notes

Human dignity originates in the act of creation. The Creator forms a soul, abundant with wisdom and goodness, in all humans who receive life in God's own image (Gn 1:26; 2:7,15). Humans, formed as both female and male, are created in relationship, a reflection of the loving unity that is the triune God. The greatness and dignity of the human person flows from communion with divine life. Human dignity is a sign of God's presence in the world.

Humans, differing in gender, are created as social beings (Gn 1:27; 2:24). Couples united in the mutual love and respect of marriage bear children. These families form together into communities and societies. Accordingly, personal growth and social development are interrelated, so that respect for the dignity of the person is fundamental in all viable societies.

The communal nature of humanity, combined with the inherent dignity of each person, are factors that contribute to the production and distribution of the world's goods. Productive activity is designed to enhance the person, both as a means for family sustenance and as a means of self-expression. The issue of dignity, then, is not a purely individual concern, but is related to the economic growth of the society. Food, clothing, shelter, everything necessary for healthy living, must be available to everyone (see *Guadium et Spes* 26 in Abbott's *The Documents of Vatican II*). People are only truly free when they can provide for their basic needs and that of their families through the exercise of self-determination. During this time of changing global economies, Pope John Paul II continually reaffirms the social teachings of the Church with its imperative standards. According to justice principles, the common good is to be the guide for the new global market. The system of economics needs to be at the service of human dignity and human rights.

In Catholic social teaching, the term *justice* has several interconnected meanings. Drawing on a dictionary definition that connects justice to truth, the Church sees the truth that Jesus demands as love, compassion, and respect. As a moral virtue, justice means to give each person what is due. Again, Catholic social teaching emphasizes that all people are due respect in light of their dignity as persons. In *Economic Justice for All,* the U.S. bishops have further delineated aspects of justice (see 68–76). According to the demands of justice, human rights must be protected, and peace must reign within human relationships. Justice protects the common good wherein everyone shares equally in the gifts of creation. *Commutative justice* calls for a fair exchange of goods and services and the honoring of commitments. *Distributive justice* requires that the basic material needs of all people be met as wealth and power are shared within society. The term *social justice* indicates that social, economic, and political structures must be organized in a manner that safeguards human rights and provides for the common good. The Church's contribution to society is to form hearts for peace, love, and justice.

Church teaching stresses that besides having basic needs met, the human person also needs free exercise of the will. Pope John Paul II indicates the importance of freedom for the transcendent dignity of the person (see *On the Hundredth Anniversary* 46). When humans are free to respond to the voice of God by doing what is good, they live a moral life that bears witness to the dignity of the person.

The reality of sin in God's perfect creation, however, means that the dignity of persons is threatened in societies throughout the world. Early peoples recorded their awareness of the sinful aspect of humanity in Genesis stories (Gn 3; 4). The twentieth-century awareness of social sin indicates that not only individuals, but also structures within society may perpetuate a demeaning of the human person. Millions suffer from poverty, hunger, and homelessness. The preservation of human dignity necessi-

tates an evaluation and restructuring of institutions and policies that perpetuate violence, oppression, and depravation. While not sanctioning any particular political system, the church approves governmental structures that safeguard human dignity. The goal of the local parish is to reflect a comprehensive concern for human life and dignity. Faith should shape actions that seek unity and avoid divisiveness and partisanship (see *Communities of Salt and Light*).

Humanity, originally created in the image of God, is definitively redeemed from its sinful state through the paschal mystery of Jesus Christ. Anyone who is in Christ is a new creation. All is new in Christ; the old order of sinful dominion has passed away (2 Cor 5:17). Jesus has given humanity the fruits of the Spirit, through which the whole of humanity is renewed. Each person becomes capable of discharging the new law of love. The indwelling Spirit demands a respect for the dignity of each person.

Human Dignity and Human Rights

Preparation Page

Purpose: To encourage members to find ways to promote respect for the dignity of all people.

Basic Materials: name tags, newsprint, markers, percussion instrument, cloth, candle, Bibles, seasonal sign, matches, pens and/or pencils, masking tape, songbooks or words reproduced with permission

Additional Materials: index cards, basket, news article about deprived human dignity, posterboard (*optional*), holy water in a bowl, an evergreen or leafy branch

Music: "Shekinah/The Temple of God" and "A Remembering Heart" from *A Remembering Heart*

Refreshments: Plan refreshments that suggest dignity in simplicity (for example, something made from corn or rice). A local shelter may provide something for a small donation or a name mention

Getting Ready: Refer to "Preparation Checklist for Each Session" to set up the room, the prayer space, and refreshment items. Add the holy water and branch to the prayer space.

■ Write the following on newsprint in list form: the name, family members, hobbies, and favorite book or movie of as many members as possible.

■ Peruse newspapers and magazines for a recent story about addiction, homelessness, prostitution, domestic abuse, or another demeaning situation.

■ *Option:* Make a poster with definitions for *justice* found in "From Our Experience." Display the poster each session.

■ Make copies of the "Human Rights Survey" handout found at the end of the session.

■ For the "Human Dignity Bingo" option, prepare the game cards from the handout at the end of this session. Make at least one card for each member. If necessary, make a copy of the sheet or add other ideas. Cut out each of the suggestions to promote dignity, and glue them onto index cards. Place the index cards in a basket.

■ As members arrive, ask a volunteer to prepare Romans 8:14–17,26–27.

■ Write the following on slips of paper, and give them to some members to say during the prayer petitions: "That we all may have a joyful greeting for everyone we meet, regardless of race or ethnic background, we pray." "That we extend a welcome to newcomers in our community, especially those new to this country, we pray." "That our parishes may serve as examples of sharing and mutual respect, we pray."

Strategy Hint: Adapt the "From Our Experience" component to a current real-life situation in your community or the greater society. Draw on current news stories, or provide a video about an issue affecting the global family. (See the resource appendix for video providers.) Use this introductory time to relate church social teachings to the daily decisions of the members.

Human Dignity and Human Rights

Session Plan Outline

Opening

Welcome. Greet members as they arrive, and hand out name tags. Invite the members to mix and get know one another by sharing the information on the newsprint: name, family members, hobbies, and favorite book or movie. Invite them to gather in a circle around the prayer space. Pointing to one person at a time, ask them all to say together the first name. Then ask the members to tell something they just learned about the person.

Gathering Prayer. Distribute the songbooks or song sheets.

Leader: **We gather together to reach into our hearts and explore how we may fully live the mission of Jesus.**

Leader: **+ Creator and giver of life, you have called us to spread the Good News of justice for all. Help us give witness to the dignity of all people. Bless our efforts to understand your way in the Spirit of Christ, our Lord.**

All: **Amen.**

All: *Sing "Shekinah/The Temple of God" from* **A Remembering Heart.**

From Our Experience

A Right to Dignity. Share a recent newspaper or magazine story about addiction, homelessness, prostitution, domestic abuse, or another situation in which human dignity is threatened. In open discussion, share the following questions:

• **What is your reaction when you read this kind of story?**

• **What other circumstances deprive persons of dignity?**

Human Dignity and Justice. Talk about the different understandings of justice. Present the term *justice* in Catholic social teaching as different from legal justice. Our bishops in *Economic Justice for All* have offered some specific understandings of justice. Include the following points, and write the highlights on newsprint or point them out on a premade poster:

• One possible dictionary definition of *justice* is "conformity to truth." The "truth" that Jesus demands includes love, compassion, respect, and care.
• Morally, justice is giving each person what is due. Since each person is due respect, rights must be protected and peace must reign.
• *Commutative justice* is the fair exchange of goods and services with respect for contracts and obligations.
• *Distributive justice* means that all people have fair access to the earth's resources to meet their basic needs.

- *Social justice* requires all social, economic, religious, and political systems to safeguard human rights, so every person can contribute freely to the common good.
- The logical vehicle of justice is love so the dignity of each person is respected.

Scripture and Tradition

From Scripture: Human Dignity. Mention that the long church tradition of safeguarding dignity is rooted in Scripture. Distribute Bibles, and divide the members into groups of four or five. Write the following references on newsprint or the board, and ask them to find what we learn about human dignity from Scripture (parenthetical statements are for the leader only)

- Genesis 1:26–27 (Created in God's image, humans are endowed with dignity.)
- Genesis 1:28 (There is dignity in responsibility for creation.)
- Psalm 8:3–7 (Dignity of humans is from God.)
- Ephesians 2:10 (Human dignity is redeemed through creation in Jesus Christ.)
- Romans 8:29 (Share in the dignity of Jesus Christ.)

Invite the members to share insights.

From Church Social Teaching: Rights and Dignity. Mention that as disciples of Christ, we carry on the church tradition of safeguarding the basic rights that promote human dignity. Pope John XXIII's encyclical *Pacem in terris: Peace on Earth* provides criteria for evaluating our social practices in light of dignity. Distribute the "Human Rights Survey" handout and pencils. Ask the participants to take five minutes to quickly read through the survey and make a slash mark at the level they believe each right is safeguarded in our society. (If it is helpful, identify the society as the local community or our nation.) Divide the members into small groups. Have them discuss which rights need better protection for the dignity of all and suggest some possible actions.

Ask for group feedback. Divide a sheet of newsprint into two columns: one for well-protected rights and one for rights that require justice work. In open discussion, ask the following questions and chart the members' responses:
- What rights are well protected in our society?
- What rights are poorly protected?
- What are some possible justice actions required?

Break. Serve refreshments that suggest a dignified, yet simple lifestyle (for example, something made from corn or rice or purchased from a self-help group).

Called to Live Justly

Choose one of the following options:

Human Dignity Bingo Option. Play "Human Dignity Bingo" made from the handout at the end of this session. Explain that each person is asked to try to perform the act of human dignity that they end up with before the next session. Randomly assign each player a number, starting with number one. Number one begins by pulling a card from the basket and reading it. Number two has the option of taking the card from number one or choosing another and reading it. When a player's card is taken, that player draws and reads the new card. Number three can choose a new card and read it or take one from one of the others. Each member will leave with one suggestion for promoting human dignity. Distribute pencils, and have them write their names on the back of their cards.

One Specific Action Option. Together summarize some insights about human dignity. Ask each member to think of one specific action they may take to help further respect for all. Ask them to pray for the efforts of one another through the week. Pass out index cards and pencils so they can write down their intention. Have them write their names on the backs.

Group Prayer

Explain that as prayer begins, each member will place their cards with the name side up in the basket and pick up a Bible for Psalm 146:5–10. Indicate the order of prayer and side one and side two to alternate verses for the psalm. Strike the percussion instrument, and light the candle.

Leader: Lord God, Creator of humanity, you made each of us in your image, the image of love and compassion, and you call us to protect the rights of all people. We listen to your wisdom and respond with loving and open hearts as we strive to do your will. Please continue inspiring us to contribute to the dignity of all people.

Reader: *Proclaims Romans 8:14–17,26–27 and concludes with, "The word of the Lord."*

All: Thanks be to God.

Silence

All: *Pray Psalm 146:5–10, alternating verses by designated sides.*

Leader: We place our petitions before our loving God and ask that the dignity of each person be safeguarded. Please respond to the following with, "Lord, let your Spirit move us."

Begin with the first petition. Those with prepared slips continue.

That we may strive to protect the dignity of all, we pray.

That we all may have a joyful greeting for everyone we meet, regardless of race or ethnic background, we pray.

That we extend a welcome to newcomers in our community, especially those new to this country, we pray.

That our parishes may serve as examples of sharing and mutual respect, we pray.

Invite other petitions by making a hand gesture.

Leader: O God, you hear all our prayers, those spoken and those held in our hearts. We offer ourselves as your servants to spread dignity for all.

Leader: *(sprinkles intention cards)* O God of Jacob, God of Mercy, bless our intentions to help others gain respect and dignity. *(sprinkles the people)* Bless each of us, that we may be leaven in our families, with our friends, and in our workplaces, so that all will come to a deep respect for one another.

All: Amen.

Leader: Glory to God in the highest, and to Jesus Christ, our redeemer, whose Spirit dwells among us. Enkindle in our hearts a love for all humanity, especially the poor and oppressed. Arouse in your faithful ones a hunger and thirst for social justice and mercy. Make us, O Lord, instruments of your peace in our souls, in our families, in our country, and in our world.

All: Amen.

All: *Sing "A Remembering Heart" from* A Remembering Heart.

Leader: Let us go forth to love and serve as we offer one another a sign of peace.

Invite members to pick up their cards to take with them.

Human Rights Survey

*I*n his encyclical *Peace on Earth*, John XXIII makes the connection between human rights and duties and dignity. Every person is endowed with a free will, and universal rights and obligations are inviolable. This survey summarizes those rights. Rank the extent each right is safeguarded for all members of our society. Consider the subtle forces that keep people from exercising their rights fully. Mark 1 for lowest and 10 for highest. Discuss actions that we as individuals or as a parish could take to promote human dignity.

1. The right to life and its necessities, including food, clothing, shelter, medical care, and social services:

   Safeguarded in our society   1 2 3 4 5 6 7 8 9 10

2. The right to preserve one's cultural and moral values:

   Safeguarded in our society   1 2 3 4 5 6 7 8 9 10

3. The rights to personal respect, to express opinions, and to be truthfully informed:

   Safeguarded in our society   1 2 3 4 5 6 7 8 9 10

4. The right to an education:

   Safeguarded in our society   1 2 3 4 5 6 7 8 9 10

5. The right to worship the Absolute:

   Safeguarded in our society   1 2 3 4 5 6 7 8 9 10

6. The right to freely choose one's state in life and to support and educate a family:

   Safeguarded in our society   1 2 3 4 5 6 7 8 9 10

7. The right for the opportunity to work, including healthy and moral conditions, a just wage, and adaptions for parenthood:

   Safeguarded in our society   1 2 3 4 5 6 7 8 9 10

8. The right to the fruits of one's labor:

   Safeguarded in our society   1 2 3 4 5 6 7 8 9 10

9. The right to assemble and establish associations:

   Safeguarded in our society   1 2 3 4 5 6 7 8 9 10

10. The right to emigrate and immigrate:

    Safeguarded in our society   1 2 3 4 5 6 7 8 9 10

11. The rights to take an active part in public affairs and to juridical protection:

    Safeguarded in our society   1 2 3 4 5 6 7 8 9 10

Acts to Promote Human Dignity

Choose one day to smile at everyone you meet.	Ask friends for soap and shampoo samples for a homeless shelter.
Really listen to someone whose point of view you do not agree with. Don't argue.	Visit an elderly person.
Do something to encourage on-site day care for working mothers.	Offer to direct an activity at a care home.
Find out about other religious practices.	Clean out a closet, and give good clothes to St. Vincent de Paul or another agency.
Read or watch public television about a crisis situation.	Do something to make an immigrant feel welcome.
Evaluate a television program for its attitudes about human dignity.	Find out how volunteers help in schools.
In church or elsewhere, sit next to someone who normally sits alone.	Say, "Have a nice day" at the end of every conversation for one day.
Learn five words of a new language.	Pray daily for a greater respect for human dignity.
Give a needed item to a care agency.	Pray daily for mothers who need to work.
Visit a council or board meeting of the city, school, or county.	Pray daily for more moral messages in the media.
Give a box of diapers to a women's shelter.	Pray a blessing for the field workers and farmers who make our food possible.
Develop an address list of legislators.	Help a food kitchen or pantry.
Surf the World Wide Web for organizations that seek dignity for all.	

Solidarity

Background Notes

The principle of solidarity calls believers to see every other human being as an equal with all the rights, responsibilities, and dignity to which each person is entitled. Pope John Paul II assigned a moral status to the principle of solidarity (see *On Social Concern* 38). As an imperative, not an option, the commitment to solidarity must be developed as an attitude and exercised as a virtue. The document clarifies that solidarity is more a than a feeling of compassion or the desire to give to charity. It is an ongoing conversion calling the believer to persevering commitment to the common good. Purposeful activities that are designed to give people sensitizing experiences of others' conditions generate attitudes of solidarity. Consciousness is raised for mainstream members of society through personal contact with the poor, the oppressed, and the needy in a manner that heightens sensitivity and brings them to a change of heart.

The principle of solidarity emerges from the Christian understanding of the Trinitarian God. Persons are formed in God's image to abide in a love relationship with others. Modeling by word and deed, Christ identifies with the hungry, the rejected, the outcast, and the poor and calls believers to treat them the same (Mt 25:40). The Body of Christ encompasses all God's children in union with the Holy Being throughout the world, so when one member suffers, all suffer with that member, as when one is honored, all rejoice (1 Cor 12:26). In that Christ calls all friends, all people are called to a giving and supportive friendship.

God in wisdom created humans in families, and thus, the call to solidarity begins in the home. When family members treat each other with dignity and respect, they form the first links of solidarity. When they appreciate one anothers' gifts and contributions, they form attitudes of solidarity. When they help one another in need, they perform small acts of solidarity. Solidarity is essentially the will to treat every person as a beloved family member.

By extension, the parish family provides experiences to stimulate awareness and attitudes of solidarity. Today's parishes, as welcoming places for immigrants, provide a venue for believers to learn about a diversity of traditions and customs. Parish announcements can include statistics about hunger, human rights, or oppressive companies. Missionary speakers and video nights are possibilities to stimulate an interest in the worldwide situation for those who otherwise would remain complacent. The sacramental life of the parish helps form Catholics into a solidarity people, who recognize the personhood of each and every human, so there are no longer the divisions of Greek or Jew, slave or free, man or woman, rich or poor, but one Body of Christ (Gal 3:28). The one loaf carries the meaning of the one Body, complete with outcasts and the marginalized, and eliminates any "them" and "us" attitudes. In a healthy body, each of the members thrives in interdependence, each has a responsibility to the others, and all, rich and poor, sit at the same table. In their recent synod, the American bishops asked for an increased solidarity among the churches of both Americas. Believers, as individuals, as peoples, and as nations, are called to see the "other" as a neighbor, not someone to be exploited. All are equal sharers at the table, for when we make others' problems and struggles our own, true communion results.

Moreover, eucharistic sharing is accompanied by forgiveness and reconciliation. Believers are called to love their neighbors, even their enemies, as Jesus loves everyone. All must be ready to sacrifice, even to the point of death (1 Jn 3:16), forsaking all prejudices and selfish interest. When individuals feel the pain of others, they become willing to make sacrifices to relieve the suffering. In the interest of others, they give spontaneously from their own income and time to generate relief. Solidarity is achieved

---

when individuals and groups break through the walls of division and emerge with a respect for the diversity within the human family.

While solidarity naturally leads to actions on behalf on the poor and suffering, it is more than a sense of charity. It is certain that those who are more able provide inspiration, support, and hope, so those who are oppressed in some way may gain strength to take action themselves. Intermediary subgroups within society are called to put aside selfish interests and strive for goals that respect the common interests of all. Believers are called to own the struggles of others.

Although the path of solidarity can sometimes seem insurmountable, defeat is never an acceptable response. While solidarity brings an enjoyment of new music, art, stories, and traditions, that joy is overshadowed by the haunting realization of the millions who are suffering from hunger and oppression. The horror of so much suffering can be overwhelming, and the reality of sin and feelings of pessimism and defeat can tempt people away from action. However, with courageous hope, believers, together and sustained by prayer, are the instruments of miracles in the world. Much has been accomplished already, a sign that much more can be done.

The exercise of solidarity yields many fruits. The experience of mutual respect and understanding are the foundational steps to peace in the world. The sharing and cooperation realized through solidarity will lead to a change away from unjust economic and international structures toward equality and respect for human rights. Mutual distrust is transformed into interdependence and collaboration, which leads to peace. Furthermore, the call to solidarity is a call to inclusive language that generates attitudes of equality. As men and women begin to see others as true equals in the eye of God, women's status will be elevated, and the multitude of oppressive conditions for women will diminish. Accordingly, children throughout the world will be respected as models of heavenly citizenship, as in "Let the children come to me," because such is the domain of God (Mt 19:14). In short, those who experience solidarity are called to respect the rights of all: workers rights, political rights, the right to determine one's own lifestyle, the right to free expression. In experiencing solidarity, believers are drawn to simplify their own lifestyles to live in identity with those who have less. Additionally, by reducing personal expenses, believers will have more funds available for social justice causes. In their struggle to bring good out of evil, believers recognize the limitations of human capabilities and come to rely on the God of salvation. We are not waiting passively for a future day when good will eventually triumph over sinful structures. Believers realize that the new human family is growing here and now among those who express the concrete demands of faith—a just and necessary transformation of the world.

Solidarity

Preparation Page

Purpose: To promote the principle of solidarity as advocated in Catholic social teaching.

Basic Materials: name tags, newsprint, markers, percussion instrument, cloth, candle, Bibles, seasonal sign, matches, pens or pencils, masking tape, songbooks or words reproduced with permission

Additional Materials: world wall-map, removable adhesive color dots, three baskets or plastic tubs, heat-proof containers with sand in the bottom, incense, incense charcoal (from a religious supply store), items from various cultures (for example, clothing, crafts, instruments), rain stick (*optional*)

Music: "Gather Us O God" from *A Remembering Heart* and "People of Passion" from *A Eucharistic People*

Refreshments: Ahead of the session, call some participants and ask them to bring foods that represent their heritages.

Getting Ready: Refer to "Preparation Checklist for Each Session" to set up the room, the prayer space, and refreshment items.

■ Place items from various cultures around the room and prayer space.

■ Display the wall map. Place nearby three colors of adhesive dots into three containers labeled "family origins," "friend and neighbor origins," and "little or no personal connection."

■ Place a piece of incense charcoal on top of sand in a heat-proof container. Just before the session begins, light the charcoal and place the incense nearby.

■ Print Psalm 86:1–2,5–6,9–10,15–16 on newsprint.

■ Plan to ask volunteers to prepare Luke 10:25–37 and 1 Corinthians 12:24–27.

■ Make copies of the "Solidarity" and "A Dozen Ways to Promote Solidarity" handouts found at the end of this session.

Strategy Hint: Be aware of controversial issues that may touch members on a personal level or stimulate conflicting opinions. Members should be cautioned that the right to differ is an important aspect of human dignity. No member should be the target of blame or be made to feel guilty. The leader should facilitate the discussion so all comments are directed to the entire group, with respect given to all points of view. The leader should restate all opinions in positive terms that strive for solutions.

Solidarity

Session Plan Outline

Opening

Welcome. Greet everyone, and invite them to put on a name tag. Explain to the first people who arrive that three colors of adhesive dots may be placed on the map according to the following categories: countries of family origins, countries of origin of friends and neighbors, and some countries with little or no personal connection.

Have them invite others, as they arrive, to add to the map and talk about their choices.

Gathering Prayer. When all participants have had an opportunity to share, invite them to gather around the prayer table by striking an instrument. Distribute songbooks or words printed with permission. Indicate the order of prayer and sides one and two to alternate reading Psalm 86:1–2,5–6,9–10,15–16 from the newsprint.

All: *Sing "Gather Us O God" from* A Remembering Heart.

Leader: + (*Sprinkle incense on the hot charcoal and lift the container high.*)

O Divine Justice, we come here seeking knowledge and understanding so that we may live in joy with your people. (*Lower the container towards the ground with a sweeping motion.*) Bless this ground on which we stand. May we draw strength and courage from it as the wise ones who have walked here before us did. (*Hold the container at mid-level, and sweep the incense toward the members.*) Send your holy breath upon us, and open us to one another. Teach us to live humbly with one another, all as equals on your holy planet, earth. (*Set the incense on a fireproof surface in the middle of the group.*)

Together we offer a prayer of the ages. (*With a hand motion, have side one begin the psalm.*)

All: *Pray Psalm 86:1–2,5–6,9–10,15–16.*

Leader: O Holy Spirit, guide us as we learn. Jesus, be with us as we grow together. We end our prayer. +

All: Amen.

From Our Experience

Identifying with Others. Say the following or similar words:

We gather today to continue our exploration of Catholic social teaching. Our bishops, together with Pope John Paul II, have asked us to live in solidarity with our neighbors, both locally and throughout the world. To some degree, we each already live in solidarity with others. Please take a few moments to share answers with a person next to you.

Option: Write the following questions on newsprint, and discuss the answers.
- What countries and cultures do I identify with, and how do I express that identity (for example, language, foods, music, travel, letter exchange)?
- What countries and cultures do I need to learn more about?

Scripture and Tradition

From Scripture: Samaritan Story Revisited. Invite the reader to proclaim Luke 10:25–37. Say the following or similar words:

> Let's look at the story of the good Samaritan with a new eye. We're accustomed to using this parable as our inspiration for being a good Samaritan for others, to find ways to help those in need. How often do we think of ourselves as the ones in need? The Samaritan was a foreigner journeying in a hostile country, who was despised for having strange cultural and faith practices.

Divide into groups of four or five to discuss the following questions. Write these questions on newsprint.
- Who are the "Samaritans" in our country, community, and parish, the ones who are in a foreign land and who come with their own special cultural practices?
- What gifts do they bring? What services do they provide for others?
- How do they make our country better with their presence? What can we all learn from the faith practices and cultural values brought here by immigrants?

From Church Social Teaching: One Human Family. Distribute the "Solidarity" handout. Say the following or similar words:

> Whenever we learn to appreciate the values of and respect the dignity of others, we grow in solidarity as one human family. Let's look at some statements from Church social teaching. The call to solidarity is examined in Pope John Paul II's encyclical *On Social Concern*. In small groups, consider the statements from the encyclical, and discuss the questions.

Break. Share refreshments that represent a variety of cultures.

Called to Live Justly

Discuss ways to live as a parish with more solidarity. Consider the following ideas or suggest others. List the ideas on newsprint. (Use the information in parentheses to obtain more information on the chosen topic.) Suggest the group choose a concrete action and form an ad hoc committee of those interested. Assign a volunteer to get the information, and set a date to plan the next step.

- Sponsor a Work of Human Hands sale (call 800-685-7572).
- As a parish or as individuals, join Catholic Charities (write to Catholic Charities USA at 1731 King Street, Suite 200, Alexandria VA 22314).
- If one does not exist locally, establish a hospitality committee that welcomes newcomers and helps them adjust. If there is a need, offer citizenship classes (for information about Pastoral Care of Migrants and Refugees, call 202-541-3230).
- Find out about diocesan global solidarity partnerships or parish twinning (call 410-625-2220, extension 3235, or contact Catholic Relief Services; for the Haiti Parish Twinning Program, call 615-356-5999.)
- Offer a mission awareness catechetical series (call The Columban Fathers' Mission Education Office, 402-291-1920, for free loan materials).

Distribute the handout "A Dozen Ways to Promote Solidarity" for members to refer to at home. Together identify some solidarity issues, and commit to pray for improvement in these areas.

Group Prayer

Ask the members to gather around the prayer table with the solidarity petitions prepared during the small group discussion (see number five on the "Solidarity" handout). Use a rain stick or an instrument that expresses another culture to call the members to prayer.

Leader: Let us pray in solidarity with all peoples, that we all may become more aware of the diverse needs of others.

Reader: *Proclaims 1 Corinthians 12:24b–27.*

Leader: O Triune God, by your very nature, you have shown us your desire that we live in a relationship of love as one family. So we place before you our petitions, that you may help us achieve unity. (*Invite members to offer the petitions formed in small group discussion earlier.*)

All: *Sing "People of Passion" from* A Eucharistic People.

Leader: Glory to God in the highest, and to Jesus Christ, our redeemer, whose Spirit dwells among us. Enkindle in our hearts a love for all humanity, especially the poor and oppressed. Arouse in your faithful ones a hunger and thirst for social justice and mercy. Make us, O Lord, instruments of your peace in our souls, in our families, in our country, and in our world.

All: Amen.

Leader: Let us go forth to love and serve as we offer each other a sign of peace.

Solidarity

From John Paul II, *On Social Concern* (referred to as SRS [*Sollicitudo Rei Socialis: On Social Concern*]):

1. "It is already possible to point to the positive and moral value of the growing awareness of *interdependence* among individuals and nations ... in the contemporary world, in its economic, cultural, political, and religious elements ..." (SRS 38). Considering economic, cultural, political, and religious elements, suggest an example of global interdependence.

2. "As a 'virtue' ... *solidarity* ... is not a feeling of vague compassion or shallow distress at the misfortunes of so many people ... it is a *firm and persevering determination* to commit oneself to the *common good*; that is to say to the good of all and of each individual ... " (SRS 38). Identify a misfortune that stirs in us feelings of compassion and distress. What are some actions that can be taken to change these feelings into a firm commitment to the common good of all?

3. "Solidarity helps us to see the 'other'—whether a person, people, or nation—not just as some kind of instrument with a work capacity and physical strength to be exploited at low cost and then discarded ... [but] a sharer, on a par with ourselves, in the banquet of life to which all are equally invited by God" (SRS 39). Who are some people in the nation and in the world who are exploited because they are not considered to be equal with others?

4. "*Solidarity* is undoubtedly a Christian virtue. ... One's neighbor must therefore be loved, even if an enemy, with the same love with which the Lord loves him or her; and for the person's sake one must be ready for sacrifice, even the ultimate one: to lay down one's life ... (cf. 1 Jn 3:16)" (SRS 40). What are some sacrifices we are challenged to make to live in solidarity with all?

5. "There is discerned in the light of faith a new *model* of the *unity* of the human race, which must ultimately inspire our *solidarity*. This supreme *model of unity*, which is a reflection of the intimate life of God, one God in three Persons, is what we Christians mean by the word *communion*" (SRS 40). Write a prayer petition that expresses a desire for the unity of the human race, that all may live in intimate communion.

A Dozen Ways to Promote Solidarity

1. Pray for worldwide concerns.

2. Watch newscasts and read newspapers.

3. Check out the World Wide Web:
   - www.st.columban.org/mission_ed
   - www.catholicrelief.org
   - www.claretianpubs.org
   - www.maryknoll.org
   - www.salesianmissions.org

4. Join an organization that promotes global concerns, and read their newsletter.

5. Find out about twinning with a parish in another country.

6. Travel to learn about other people and cultures.

7. Attend cultural days and bazaars offered in the community.

8. Learn another language, listen to the music, and enjoy the crafts of other cultures.

9. Purchase goods from self-help groups, such as Work of Human Hands (800-685-7572).

10. Invest in firms with a reputation for global concern.

11. Borrow missionary videos from the diocese resource center.

12. Host a missionary, and listen to his or her story.

The Common Good, Subsidiarity, And Responsibilities

Background Notes

The goal of Catholic social teaching is to promote the common good, whereby every member of the world society enjoys a share in the products and services that enhance life. The common good includes all the social conditions that contribute—body and soul—to a person's eternal salvation. The common good is safeguarded only when every authority respects the rights that flow from the dignity of every person. As society develops ever more complex structures, personal and social responsibilities to protect the common good increase. Individuals, families, various organizations, and governments are all required to seek the common good, which is attained when the basic needs of every individual are met. These needs are not only physical but also include spiritual, psychological, and cultural well-being. The principle that orders corresponding rights and responsibilities for the common good is known as *subsidiarity*. This principle, as delineated by Pope Pius XI, assures that no broad governmental authority assumes the duties of a smaller unit (see *After Forty Years* 80). In *Economic Justice for All*, the U.S. bishops fully examine how subsidiarity needs to be the guiding principle for all the complex structures of society. They call for good government that directs, urges, and regulates the economy to truly help other groups contribute to the common good (124). Human dignity is respected when each individual or small group in society retains responsibilities and when the broader group enacts policies that ensure the rights of all. For subsidiarity to abide, individuals and families retain as many responsibilities as possible. Governments direct economic, social, and political systems to enable citizens to exercise personal duties. Since individuals are born into and form their first relationship in families, they are the basic unit of society, whose health is a crucial component of the common good. When family life is sound, individuals are empowered to employ their gifts for the benefit of the entire society; therefore, all of society's structures need to support family life. Conversely, any systems that work to the determent of families are inherently immoral. Additionally, governments and other institutions must assume the duties that cannot realistically be performed by individuals, families, or small groups. Some areas that require the support of the greater society are transportation systems, health and education guarantees for all children, and commerce regulation. Although subsidiarity recognizes an ordering of society that includes the individual, family, and governmental systems, a variety of organizations contribute to the complex system of rights and responsibilities. Businesses, charitable associations, and professional and service institutions are obliged to follow policies that enhance family life and support the common good of all. Subsidiarity, as Pope John XXIII indicated, unfortunately often breaks down at the international level, at which adequate structures to protect the common good are lacking (see *Peace on Earth* 140). Believers need to find means, while exercising precautions against further oppression, to impact unjust governments that currently do not allow freedom in rights and responsibilities.

Catholic social teaching, while promoting the well-being of all, recognizes a special consideration for the poor and suffering at all levels of decision-making. Individuals are called to make choices, not just for their own benefits and those close to them, but in a fashion that brings a more fair distribution of goods to those suffering poverty. Applying the principle of subsidiarity, Christians working together can channel the social, economic, political, cultural, and religious systems for the common good. The church, as an instrument of sal-

vation, is also subject to the principle of subsidiarity, with a responsibility to those whose rights and duties have not been safeguarded. As a worldwide organization, the church is in a position to impact sinful structures that perpetuate injustice.

Although believers are called to be active in the political realm, the church is never to be partisan. In light of the principle of subsidiarity, the local parish, a justice group, or other similar organizations should not impose decisions that are properly left to individual choices by its members. Justice seekers need to respect the fine line between calling others to social awareness and the temptation to promote favorite causes. The church assists in conscience formation and in information distribution; however, subsidiarity demands that each citizen retains the right and duty to exercise political freedom. For the church or any other body to impose a political stance on an individual is contrary to the principle of subsidiarity. Each parish community needs a pro-

cess for brainstorming, researching, and praying to help members make responsible choices. With proper encouragement that is never coercion, believers do seek the common good and insist on government and economic policies that protect human dignity.

Because the voice of citizens can have a strong influence on government, the right to vote is a crucial responsibility for believers and a necessary component of subsidiarity. The common good may be protected by an informed and active electorate. The parish community has a responsibility to immigrants who may need assistance and encouragement in the naturalization process, so that they, too, will have a voice and can exercise their responsibility in joint decision-making.

Applying the principle of subsidiarity, believers work for just systems that safeguard the rights and responsibilities of all. Through responsible citizenship, the common good is protected.

The Common Good, Subsidiarity, and Responsibilities

Preparation Page

Purpose: To foster the principle of subsidiarity for the sake of families and the common good.

Basic Materials: name tags, newsprint, markers, percussion instrument, cloth, candle, Bibles, seasonal sign, matches, pens or pencils, masking tape, songbooks or words reproduced with permission

Additional Materials: paper, votive candles for each member

Music: "So Much More" from *A Remembering Heart*

Refreshments: Call some members, and ask them to bring a refreshment to share that is a favorite in their family traditions.

Getting Ready: Refer to "Preparation Checklist for Each Session" to set up the room, the prayer space, and refreshment items.

■ Choose which options to use during the session.

■ Plan to ask volunteers to prepare to proclaim 1 Samuel 8:6–18, Isaiah 10:1–3, and Acts 15:28.

■ Place the votive candles on or near the prayer table.

■ Make copies of the two-sided handout "Subsidiarity and the Common Good" found at the end of the session.

■ Plan to ask a volunteer to prepare Isaiah 10:1–2.

Strategy Hint: Balance discussion time with other aspects of the session. Break time is important for community bonding. Members who wish to may continue talking together about the topic over refreshments. Prayer experiences are equally important to connect our efforts to the will of the Almighty, so they should not be rushed or omitted.

The Common Good, Subsidiarity, and Responsibilities

Session Plan Outline

Opening

Welcome. Greet the members as they arrive. Invite them to put on a name tag. Offer paper and markers. Explain to the first who arrive to draw diagrams of their families. (Be sensitive to those without family and immediately suggest they draw connections with friends or neighbors.) Have them encourage others as they arrive to do the same. Ask all who wish to talk about their families.

Gathering Prayer. After an appropriate time, strike a percussion instrument as a call to prayer. With a hand motion, invite all the participants to gather around the table. Distribute the songbooks or other singing aid and Bibles. Indicate the order of prayer and side one and side two to alternate verses 137–144 of Psalm 119. Light the candle.

Leader: **We gather in the name of the Father and of the Son and of the Holy Spirit. Amen. God of right relationships, we thank you for our families, our friends, and communities. Teach us how to safeguard the rights and responsibilities of each level of society. Help us find ways to strengthen the family unit. Give us wisdom to seek just laws and the courage to struggle for the common good.**

We call on the wisdom of the ages as we proclaim a desire for righteousness.

Let us pray Psalm 119. (*With a hand motion, have side one begin, alternating verses 137–144.*)

O Righteous God, you call us to seek laws that protect our families, our communities, and our world. Guide us today as we strive to understand your church's teachings of subsidiarity and the common good, so none will be unjustly controlled and so liberty will be guaranteed for all.

All: *Sing "So Much More" from* **A Remembering Heart.**

From Our Experience

Choose one of the following options.

Families in Crisis Option. Distribute pencils and paper. Ask the members to jot down their guesses to the following questions about families and children in the United States. Emphasize that this is an information survey, and correct answers are not the issue. After the survey, give the figures in parentheses, and discuss the needs of families in our society. (The following data is from the Children's Defense Fund, 2000. Their website is www.childrensdefense.org.)

- What percent of families have work income but live in legal poverty? (*8.3 percent*)

- What percent of children will live in poverty at some time? (*33 percent*)

- What percent of infants have a working mother? (*60 percent*)

- What is the average annual income of a three-person poor family? (*$9,000*)

- What percent of a poor family's income is from welfare? (*17 percent*)

- What percent of fourth-graders do not read at a basic level? (*38 percent*)

- What percent of children without health insurance are from working families? (*90 percent*)

- How many children every day are homicide victims? (*13*)

- How many children are arrested daily for violent crimes? (*280*)

- Where does the United States rank in millionaires, billionaires, and military exports? (*1st*)

Offer the statistics, and together, draw some conclusions about the family and U.S. society. Conclude that the family is the foundational unit of society. The level of function or dysfunction of families depends on the other systems within the society.

Responsibilities Option. Make three columns on newsprint, titled Family, Community, and State/Federal. Brainstorm about the following questions together and list responses in the corresponding columns.

- **What are the responsibilities of the community to the family? (for example, educational opportunities, health-care facilities, safety)**

- **What responsibilities are reserved by the family? (for example, educational choices, where to live, religious practices)**

- **What are some responsibilities delegated to state or national governments because alone, neither the family nor the local community can provide for them? (for example, health-care guarantees, just wages, environmental protection, international trade policies)**

Scripture and Tradition

From Scripture. Ask a member to proclaim each Scripture below. After each reading, ask the following question, and write key responses on newsprint.

Have a reader proclaim 1 Samuel 8:6–18.

- **What are some implications about absolute government?**

Have a reader proclaim Isaiah 10:1–3.

- **What is the caution about laws and justice?**

Have a reader proclaim Acts 15:28.

- **What do we learn about placing unnecessary legal obligations on people?**

Form some conclusions from the readings (for example, governments and institutions should not impose unjust regulations that harm, rather than nurture, the people).

From Church Teaching: Subsidiarity. Divide members into groups of five or six. Distribute the "Subsidiarity and the Common Good" handout. Ask the groups to read the summaries together and discuss the questions. After fifteen minutes, ask each group to report a main insight regarding the last question.

A Definition of Subsidiarity. Help the group develop the following or a similar definition of subsidiarity:
- The larger unit does not assume the responsibilities that belong to the smaller unit, and the purpose of government is to provide protection and services for individuals and families.

Voting and Subsidiarity. Ask for member input to connect voting responsibility to subsidiarity. Include the following points:
- Political involvement helps to maintain subsidiarity, which in turn can provide for the common good.
- The right to vote can keep larger governments from usurping the rights of the person and family and provides regulations for healthy living in the community.

Break. Invite the members to share their family tradition refreshments.

Called to Live Justly

Summarize. Invite the members to express some aspects of the principle of subsidiarity while writing the following or similar points on newsprint:
- No authority should assume the responsibilities of the smaller body.
- The role of the wider authority is to establish regulations to ensure the rights of the individual are protected.
- The more powerful authority should not impose itself unnecessarily on the smaller unit.
- Consequently, power is decentralized, while basic rights are protected.
- Voting rights are vital to the process.

Subsidiarity and the Common Good Simulation Option. Divide the participants into groups of five or six. Ask each group member to assume the role of one of the following: a family member who lives at the poverty level, local Church community member, local governing body representative (for example, the school board or city council), business person, and state and/or federal government official.

Assign an issue suggested during the previous discussion or one of the following: education, affordable housing, welfare services, work and trade issues, or immigration. Depending on local interests, assign the same topic for all the groups or a different topic for each group. Using the principle of subsidiarity, ask the members of each group to discuss the issue from the point of view of their assumed roles. After ten minutes, ask each group to share insights.

Decision to Act Option. In pairs, have the members choose an aspect of society in which the principle of subsidiarity is currently lacking or weak. Have them offer an effort they will try in the upcoming month to promote subsidiarity.

Group Prayer

Call the members to prayer by striking the percussion instrument. Explain the order of prayer. Demonstrate that at the appointed time, they may come forward to light a candle and offer an action they would like to take (for example, attend a school board meeting, write to a legislator, talk to the parish council about offering citizenship classes, or pray for subsidiarity). Light the large candle.

Leader: + O great and benevolent God, you who are perfect relationship. Thank you for showing us how to live in right order and for governments that protect the rights of children and families. We offer our prayer for the common good of all, through the Spirit and in Jesus' name.

All: Amen.

Reader: *Proclaims Isaiah 10:1–2.*

Leader: Please respond to the following with, "God of Justice, hear us."

That legislators will enact laws to protect the health and welfare of children and families, we pray.

That we will help immigrants gain citizenship with its corresponding rights and responsibilities, we pray.

That voters exercise their responsibility in a manner that helps the poor and needy, we pray.

Please take turns coming forward and lighting a small candle. (*Show how to hold the candle upward while stating their hope for subsidiarity.*)

O God, please guide us in ways that help all people live in dignity.

Glory to God in the highest, and to Jesus Christ, our redeemer, whose Spirit dwells among us. Enkindle in our hearts a love for all humanity, especially the poor and oppressed. Arouse in your faithful ones a hunger and thirst for social justice and mercy. Make us, O Lord, instruments of your peace in our souls, in our families, in our country, and in our world.

All: Amen.

Leader: Let us go forth to love and serve as we offer one another a sign of peace. Suggest that the members use their candles at home and pray for all to seek the common good.

Subsidiarity and the Common Good

Subsidiarity is a bifold principle. On one side, the rights of every individual are to be protected by the society's structures. On the other hand, these governments and organizations are not to take over the responsibilities of individuals and families. The common good is ensured when the dignity of each person is safeguarded and the functions of society—economic, political, religious, and cultural—contribute to all members reaching their full potential.

Step 1: Read over the following summaries from Catholic social teaching. Without pausing for discussion, have four members of the group each read one of the following summaries aloud.

A. Based on the principle of subsidiarity, "it is an injustice and at the same time a grave evil and a disturbance of right order" for the larger governing body to assume the "functions which can be performed and provided for by" individuals or small units (*Christianity and Social Progress* 53).

B. According to the principle of subsidiarity, "families, neighborhoods, church congregations, community organizations, civic and business associations, public interest and advocacy groups, community development corporations, and many other bodies ... play a crucial role in generating creative partnerships for the pursuit of the public good ..." (*Economic Justice for All* 308).

C. The principle of subsidiarity is missing in the current structures of world order. The universal common good suffers when no government is able "to intervene in the economy when basic justice requires greater social coordination and regulation ..." (*Economic Justice for All* 323).

D. All Catholics are called on to be voting citizens. The principle of subsidiarity depends on active, informed citizen participation in harmony with the Gospel. "For Catholics, public virtue is as important as private virtue in building up the common good. ... Participation in the political process is a moral obligation" (*Faithful Citizenship: Civic Responsibility for a New Millennium, page 9*).

Step 2: Consider the common good and the principle of subsidiarity when discussing the following questions.

1. What are some rights of families and members of society?

2. What are some individual and family responsibilities?

3. According to Catholic social teaching, what is the role of government and organizations regarding the public good?

4. To what current issues could the principle of subsidiarity and the common good apply?

Stewardship, the Poor, and the Environment

Background Notes

"Think! The heavens, even the highest heavens, belong to the LORD, your God, as well as the earth and everything on it" (Dt 10:14).

Stewardship, the use of one's time, treasure, and talent for the benefit of all, applies to both local and global issues. The imperative is not satisfied by contributions made to our own communities or only from our excess. Furthermore, stewardship involves more than charity. Believers are called to be responsible citizens and consumers. A responsible consumer seeks just compensation for laborers, a fair distribution of the world's products, and protection of the earth's resources for the common good of all.

Human beings, as created in the image of God, are given dominion (Gn 1:26), with a commission to use their creative powers to cultivate and care for the earth (Gn 2:15). Through labor, humans enhance natural resources so products may exist in abundance for all. Justice demands that resources be equally available so all persons, in present and future generations, may share responsibly in the earth's bounty. Dominion (Gn 1:28) is never exploitation for the accumulation of wealth. Believers are cautioned in Scripture against the love of money and riches (1 Tm 6:6–10). People are empowered to work productively, not so they can acquire an excess of riches, but so there is plenty to share.

Because justice demands that all persons be allowed an enhanced life through a fair share of the world's products, the common good must be the priority in the distribution of all commodities (see *Gaudium et Spes* 69 regarding the rightful possession and use of earthly goods by all). The principle of stewardship recognizes that people, gifted with talents and skills, are entitled to the products of their own work. Through labor, human beings obtain the goods to be used for their own well-being, to support families, and to provide for the overall common good.

Temperance, then, is the virtue that guides stewardship. When everyone practices self-discipline and moderation, there will be plenty to share now and for posterity. A spirituality of consumption calls believers to not only take precautions against their own overconsumption but also to take an active role to protect the environment and those vulnerable to exploitation. By joining together, believers can gain support from one another in their efforts to reduce, reuse, and recycle and to promote national and international policies that protect human rights and the environment. Humans, then, are entrusted to use and care for the environment in a manner that protects resources for future generations and provides for a just distribution, so all may benefit from their own labors and the land on which they reside.

According to the biblical tradition and Catholic social teaching, any society can be evaluated on how well the poor and powerless are able to live. A preference for the poor, who, in their dependency on God, are models of faith for all, is essential to stewardship. When the earth's products are being avariciously devoured by an indulging few, the expense is paid in the suffering of the many; however, God hears the cry of the oppressed (Ex 3:7–10). When products are produced in one country by oppressed labor to be sold in excess in another part of the world, believers have a responsibility to carry on Christ's work to bring relief to those in need (Lk 4:18–19). Justice requires believers to seek sufficient wages, so all workers and their families may live in dignity (see *Christianity and Social Progress* 71 for considerations of a just wage). The Gospel affirms that while the wealthy are not excluded from salvation, the poor hold a special place of honor in God's domain (Lk 4:16–21 and Lk 7:18–23).

Conscientious stewardship inspires believers to couple prudence with purchasing power and to ask some hard questions about their own consumer habits and charitable attitudes. In evaluating our

own consumption habits, we need to assess what we can do without and in which areas we are overconsuming. Additionally, modern communications enable consumers to research the source of many purchased goods. We often can find out which goods have been made available through just conditions and determine which companies are exploitive of labor or the environment in their manufacturing and distribution practices. With the widow's mite as the model (Mk 12:41–44), Christians are called to share everything, not just from their excess. Since all things belong to God (Ex 19:5; Dt 10:14), this sharing is not an act of charity, but a return to those in need that which is already theirs (see *On the Development of Peoples* 23 for a quotation from St. Ambrose).

Stewardship compels believers to impact social, economic, and political policies. Because everyone is entitled to access the goods of the earth, the faithful are called to invest time and finances to help create just systems and abolish unjust ones. These critical decisions require an awareness of worldwide situations. Fortunately, many organizations make their information readily available through newsletters, the Internet, and a variety of publications. The National Conference of Catholic Bishops, through the United States Catholic Conference, publishes materials for parish use and maintains an up-to-date website.

The international debt crisis, an issue that demands current attention, has caused extensive poverty and suffering throughout the world. Countries that have been forced to spend millions in debt maintenance have been deprived of those resources for their own infrastructures to improve their standard of living. Too often, international lenders, bankers, and affluent nations have been irresponsible in loaning large sums to unreliable leaders who have either spent the funds unwisely or pilfered them for their own indulgences. International law

should hold these leaders, and the countries who have given asylum to deposed rulers, accountable. Immediate debt relief is the only justifiable response for the people who are suffering a debt burden but have not been the benefactors of the funds. Biblical wisdom provides us with models for ending oppressive debt (Lv 25:25,28). Holding the people of a debtor nation in oppressive captivity while the present or past leaders live a life of luxury is a particularly grave injustice.

Charity is one necessary and proper aspect of stewardship. Just concern is always for the most vulnerable, who remain neglected, exploited, and marginalized when injustices and oppression replace standards of stewardship. All who are suffering from malnutrition, disease, and homelessness are entitled to immediate relief. Those who contribute should realize, however, that they are returning to those in need what is rightfully theirs and already due to them as their fair share in God's gifts of creation. The preferential option for the poor extends beyond charity, which by itself, does nothing to eliminate the cause to put an end to the suffering, to political empowerment.

Those who are more able because of fortune of birth and education are obliged to use their time and talents to help find ways to empower those born in less-fortunate circumstances. Efforts must be made to include all people in the political and economic decisions that impact their lives. Agencies with a successful record for effecting change (for example, Maryknoll, Campaign for Human Development, Salesians, Columban Fathers, Bread for the Poor) need to be supported so they can continue to establish education, health care, and grassroots systems that empower the global poor to effect changes away from unjust systems and toward self-fulfillment. In turn, all people, as just stewards no longer dependent on charity, will be able to realize the dignity that is their due.

Stewardship, the Poor, and the Environment

Preparation Page

Purpose: To call members to stewardship with a concern for the poor and the environment.

Basic Materials: name tags, newsprint, markers, percussion instrument, cloth, candle, Bibles, seasonal sign, matches, pens or pencils, masking tape, songbooks or words reproduced with permission

Additional Materials: yellow and blue index cards or substitute with colors that are available, (one of each for every player), four colors of embroidery thread cut into twelve-inch pieces (four strands for each member) *(optional)*, map or outline of continents on poster paper

Music: "To the Creator" and "We Are Called to Serve" from *A Eucharistic People*

Refreshments: Order foods from a company that fosters concern for the environment and the poor. For a catalog from Work of Human Hands, call 800-685-7572; or try www.rainforestshop .com.

Getting Ready: Refer to "Preparation Checklist for Each Session" to set up the room, the prayer space, and refreshment items.

■ Either use a purchased laminated map, or draw a simple outline of the continents on poster paper. Mount the mural of the earth on an easily accessible wall.

■ Plan to ask three volunteers to prepare Luke 4:17–19 and the alternate verses of Daniel 3:74–81 for the beginning prayer.

■ Plan to ask volunteers to prepare Genesis 1:24–31 and Matthew 11:5 for the session.

■ Make copies of the "Time, Treasures, and Talents for the Good of All" handout found at the end of the session.

■ For the group ending prayer, plan to ask four volunteers to prepare Acts 2:44–45; Proverbs 8:20–21; Matthew 11:5; and Luke 6:20. Choose the song, and have word sheets, with permission, and accompaniment.

■ Plan to ask two volunteers to be anointers, and instruct them when to pick up the oils and say to each member, "Through the work of these hands, may God's people and all creation be protected and renewed." Prepare two small containers (for example, votive candleholders) with fragrant oil. *Suggestion:* Write the above anointing phrase on two small cards and tape to the holders.

Strategy Hint: For the sake of justice, keep the sessions from being a forum for anyone's personal agenda—neither the facilitator's nor any member's. Justice requires that action choices emerge from group process, and members must not be channeled into someone's preplanned cause. Protect the group from those who want to vent about personal insults or injuries. Any member with serious personal issues should be directed to the pastor or another parish staff member who can minister to those special needs.

Stewardship, the Poor, and the Environment

Session Plan Outline

Opening

Welcome. Greet everyone as they arrive, and offer each a name tag. Invite them to trace their hands, overlapping each other, on the earth mural.

Gathering Prayer. After an appropriate time, strike a percussion instrument as a call to prayer. With a hand motion, invite all to gather around the table. Distribute the songbooks or other singing aid and Bibles. Indicate the order of prayer, teach the refrain for each verse of the Daniel reading, and then light the candle.

Leader: + O Creator God, you who made us in your image, send your Spirit upon us to teach us the true meaning of stewardship and inspire us toward the common good in using your earthly gifts. Thank you for all your bountiful blessings. We pray in Jesus' name.

All: Amen.

Reader: *Proclaims Luke 4:17–19.*

Readers: *Alternately proclaim the first half of each verse in Daniel 3:74–81, while members then say the response.*

All: Praise God above all forever.

All: *Sing "To the Creator" from* A Eucharistic People.

From Our Experience

"Who pays? Who plays?" Activity. Distribute to each member one blue and one yellow card. Assure them that the goal is not to get a right or wrong answer, but to become more aware. Explain that "Who pays?" is a short expression for "Who sacrifices something?" not who uses cash for what they want. Ask them to listen to each situation and hold up the appropriate color card in response to each question. Read the situations slowly, and repeat as necessary.

- Yellow, a child in an African country, gets $3.50 annually from the government in both health and education benefits, while Blue, international financiers, collects $17 per person for governmental debt. Who pays? Who plays?

- Blue, a legislator, relaxes on vacation at the family mountain home, while Yellow, an inner-city parent, lacks the education and training to rise above the poverty level. Who pays? Who plays?

- From the Balkan area, Yellow is among one out of every two persons who have been displaced because of Blue's struggle for power. Who pays? Who plays?

- Yellow, a pregnant woman in rural Indonesia, eats bark and roots, while Blue, a military leader, enjoys profits from investments. Who pays? Who plays?

- Blue, living in the United States, consumes 28 percent more energy than Yellow does in a less-developed country. Who pays? Who plays?

- Blue, a child in the United States, receives toys and clothes as birthday presents that are worth more than Yellow's annual income as a factory worker in Haiti, who made one of the gifts. Who pays? Who plays?

- Blue purchases a pair of jeans from a local discount store for $16, while Yellow, a woman working twelve hours a day in a Free Trade Zone factory, still cannot buy sufficient food. Who pays? Who plays?

- Yellow, among the millions who are victims of African wars, is near starvation, while Blue is a diamond broker. Who pays? Who plays?

Ask the group to draw some conclusions about the consumption of the world's goods and the need for just stewardship. Possibilities include the following:
- Yellow represents people, more often women and children, who are suffering drastic economic hardship and who do not enjoy a fair share of the earth's products.
- Blue represents those who enjoy an excess of goods produced from the world's resources, often at the expense of others.
- There exists a massive unbalance in the distribution of wealth and goods in the world.
- While the greatest disparity is between those in technologically developed countries and the rest of the world, millions also suffer within developed countries.

Conclude that for many years, stewardship was defined as how believers gave of their time, treasure, and talent to their parish communities, but global realities now demand a much broader understanding. The principle of stewardship asks Christians to take responsibility for a more just distribution of products and protection of the earth's resources.

Scripture and Tradition

From Scripture. Have readers proclaim Genesis 1:24–31 and Matthew 11:5. Discuss the responsibility of dominion and Jesus' preferential concern for the poor and needy.

Divide the members into small groups of three or four. Write the following question on newsprint:

- **What would be the implications if each biblical message were lived to the fullest?**

Assign a different passage to each group, and ask them to read and discuss it in light of the question.
- Luke 3:10–14 (Each would use only what is needed, share, and not abuse others.)
- Luke 4:16–19 (Debt and oppression would be wiped out.)
- 1 Peter 4:9–10 (Each would employ their gifts for the benefit of others.)

- Leviticus 25:35–38 (The poor in need of work and money would never be taken advantage of.)
- Acts 4:32–35 (All would sell their excess and distribute to those in need.)
- Matthew 6:19–21 (People would not horde earthly goods as treasures.)
- Deuteronomy 15:11 (Hands would be open to the poor.)

Have each group report highlights of their discussion to the whole group.

From Catholic Social Teaching: Stewardship. Explain that there are many ways to approach the challenge of stewardship. In this exercise, the members will examine some concepts expressed by Pope John Paul II in recent encyclicals and by the bishops of the United States.

Divide the members into groups of six or seven. Distribute the "Time, Treasures, and Talents for the Good of All" handout. Assign one section for each group. (For more than four groups, repeat the sections.) Ask them to read the quotation and discuss the questions.

After twenty minutes ask each group to report a summary of the third question.

Break. Serve refreshments that reflect a concern for the poor and the earth's resources.

Called to Live Justly

Choose from the following options:

Securing Stewardship Option. Distribute four strands of different colors of embroidery thread to each member. Ask them to knot the threads together and hang it at home as a reminder of the following:

1. to be a just consumer,

2. to exercise a preferential option for the poor in their decisions,

3. to be a steward of ecology, and

4. to find out more about countries that are suffering the consequences of international debt.

Option: Invite the members to weave the strands into a decoration or bracelet.

Home Survey Option. Suggest that at home, the members take a survey of goods. On their yellow cards from the "Who Pays? Who Plays?" exercise, have them write these questions:
- Where were the goods made?
- Were the workers who produced them paid a just wage?
- What resources were required, and how were they acquired?

On their blue cards have them write these questions:
- What products have I replaced just to have something "better"?
- How can I reduce consumption?
- What actions can I take to help reduce world poverty?

Group Prayer
Call the members to prayer by striking a percussion instrument. Indicate the order of prayer and the response to be said after each Scripture.

Leader: O Gracious and caring God, you have given us the use of our hands to provide for one another and to protect the earth. O Holy Spirit, help us to be wise in finding ways to protect the environment and secure healthy working conditions for all people. Let us not seek luxuries, but inspire us to make generous offerings for the sake of others. We pray in Jesus' name. Amen.

Response: We put our trust in you, O God. Help us be just stewards.

Readers: Proclaim Acts 2:44–45; Proverbs 8:20–21; Matthew 11:5; and Luke 6:20.

All: *Sing "We Are Called to Serve" from* A Eucharistic People.

Leader: *Motion the anointers to pick up the oils. As the singing continues, motion the members forward, palms up, to have their hands anointed with fragrant oil, with the anointers saying the following to each one:* "Through the work of these hands, may God's people and all creation be protected and renewed."

Using hand motions, invite the members to rub in the oil.

Glory to God in the highest, and to Jesus Christ, our redeemer, whose Spirit dwells among us. Enkindle in our hearts a love for all humanity, especially the poor and oppressed. Arouse in your faithful ones a hunger and thirst for social justice and mercy. Make us, O Lord, instruments of your peace in our souls, in our families, in our country, and in our world.

All: Amen.

Leader: Let us go forth to love and serve as we offer one another a sign of peace.

Time, Treasures, and Talents for the Good of All

Consumerism

From *On the Hundredth Anniversary of* Rerum Novarum 28 (for a fuller understanding of the relationship of consumerism and spiritual well-being, read section 28 in its totality):

> **Superdevelopment, which consists in an *excessive* availability of every kind of material goods for the benefit of certain social groups, easily makes people slaves of 'possession' and of immediate gratification. … This is the so-called civilization of 'consumption' or 'consumerism,' which involves so much throwing away or waste. … All of us experience firsthand the sad effects of this blind submission to pure consumerism: in the first place a crass materialism, and at the same time a *radical dissatisfaction* … the more one possesses the more one wants, while deeper aspirations remain unsatisfied and perhaps even stifled.**

1. How does society encourage consumers to replace objects just for the feeling of having something better?

2. How can we cut down on throwing away and waste?

3. What aspirations can we develop or seek outside of material consumption?

Ecology

From *Renewing the Earth: An Invitation to Reflection and Action on Environment in Light of Catholic Social Teaching*:

> **Stewardship implies that we must both care for creation according to standards that are not of our own making and at the same time be resourceful in finding ways to make the earth flourish. … Stewardship places upon us responsibility for the well-being of all God's creatures.**

1. Considering the well-being of all creation, what are some infractions?

2. For what worldwide environmental issues might we take more responsibility and exercise stewardship?

3. What do we know about the abuse of resources in Africa (or another continent) and the resulting widespread suffering? (To find about detrimental uses of the environment, particularly how the diamond industry fuels African wars, contact the African Faith and Justice Network at 202-832-3412 or log on to http://afjn.cua.

Preferential Option for the Poor

From *On the Hundredth Anniversary of* Rerum Novarum 57 and 58:

Preferential option for the poor is never exclusive or discriminatory. ... The church's love for the poor, which is essential for her and a part of her constant tradition, impels her to give attention to a world in which poverty is threatening to assume massive proportions in spite of technological and economic progress. In the countries of the West, different forms of poverty are being experienced by groups which live on the margins of society, by the elderly and the sick, by the victims of consumerism, and even more immediately by so many refugees and migrants.

Love for others, and in the first place love for the poor, in whom the church sees Christ himself, is made concrete in the promotion of justice.

1. What areas of the world are in desperate poverty?

2. Who are the victims of consumerism in our own country, and what accommodations are made for the elderly, the sick, refugees, and migrants?

3. What concrete actions can better promote justice for the poor? (Contact Catholic Campaign for Human Development, National Conference of Catholic Bishops/United States Catholic Conference, 3211 4th St., NE, Washington, D.C. 20017-1194, 202-541-3000.)

International Debt

From *On the Coming of the Third Millennium:*

If we recall that Jesus came to 'preach the good news to the poor' (*Mt* 11:5 *Lk* 7:22). How can we fail to lay greater emphasis on the *Church's preferential option for the poor and the outcast?* ... Thus, in the spirit of the Book of Leviticus (25:8–12), Christians will have to raise their voice on behalf of all the poor of the world, proposing the Jubilee as an appropriate time to give thought, among other things, to reducing substantially, if not canceling outright, the international debt which seriously threatens the future of many nations.

1. What do we know about the international debt situation?

2. What has been done worldwide for debt relief?

3. What can we do to promote debt relief?

Structural/Social Sin

Background Notes

The reality of sin has been a divisive and detrimental influence on history. The nature of human progress brings with it a strong temptation (see *Gaudium et Spes* 37). Genesis stories, such as Adam and Eve and Cain and Abel, attempt to deal with the reality of sinful inclinations. Furthermore, since the earliest times, the reality of sin has been understood to have a social, as well as a personal, dimension. Stories of Noah's Ark and Sodom and Gomorrah indicate the immoral nature of entire societies whose structures were permeated with sinfulness.

Scripture calls believers to respond to structural sin.* Isaiah warns, "Woe to those who enact unjust statutes and who write oppressive decrees, depriving the needy of judgment and robbing my people's poor of their rights" (Is 10:1–2a). The implication is that laws and political forms are not necessarily just and must be evaluated by the faithful for their economic and social consequences. In the New Testament, Matthew cautions Christians against the broad way (Mt 7:13), implicating the customs of society that are easy to adopt but that lead to spiritual destruction.

Guadium et Spes specifies the root of structural sin lies in the complexity of society: "For when the order of values is jumbled, and bad is mixed with the good, individuals and groups pay heed solely to their own interests, and not to those of others" (from Abbott's translation 37). Personal and social sin exist, then, in a dialectic relationship. Personal sins may involve the misuse of power and authority.

Even though collaboration in a corporate decision that results in harm or oppression of others is still in the realm of personal responsibility, institutions help shape personal thoughts, values, and actions, so decisions of members are not made independently of societal influences. Decisions of individuals create situations that, in turn, influence further decisions of others. Unjust attitudes, greed, selfishness, and alienation are bearers of social sin that eventually modify the consciousness of the people involved (see Baum 203–5 for levels of social sin). When unjust structures foster the development of abusive attitudes, anger and despair are produced in the victims who are oppressed by the selfish actions of others. The *Catechism of the Catholic Church* helps us see the relationship between social sin and personal sin:

> Thus sin makes [humans] accomplices of one another and causes concupiscence, violence, and injustice to reign among them. Sins give rise to social situations and institutions that are contrary to the divine goodness. "Structures of sin" are the expression and effect of personal sins. They lead their victims to do evil in their turn. In an analogous sense, they constitute a "social sin" (1869).

Social sin is inherited sin in that the structure of evil is built into a society that wounds people according to the station into which each is born. Social sin is steeped in the culture of a particular group. Contrary to personal sin, social sin is not produced by an act of free will. It passes distortion from generation to generation. People are denied the good and encouraged to do evil by the customs to which they are born. In other words, social sin can be committed out of blindness. Unlike personal sin, social sin produces no guilt, in spite of evil consequences. While the standard church teaching has been that sin must be a conscious act, the injustices of social

---

* The terms *social sin* and *structural sin* are often used interchangeably. Generally speaking, social sins are any sins that emerge from and permeate a society. Structural sin means types of sins that are built into the structures that create a society. These structures that form society include attitudes and belief systems. Sometimes structural sin is used in reference to specifically organized structures, such as an oppressive governmental system or promotion policies within a company that exclude certain types of people.

sin may be perpetuated unconsciously. Social sin, in fact, involves a false consciousness, wherein evil appears to be a good thing in keeping with the values of the culture.

In the modern world, there are many manifestations of social sin, such as racism and sexism, and all structural injustices inevitably lead to the oppression of certain groups for the benefit of others. These oppressions result in an economic deprivation to a greater or lesser degree. Group decisions, whether in the political or economic realm, need to be examined in light of the world complexities of oppression. To ignore the multitudes of hungry, needy, homeless, and ill is to ignore Lazarus at the gate (Lk 16:19–31) (see *On Social Concern* 42). We are called to take action and reverse the current effects of long-term structural ills by seeking a more just distribution of the earth's goods. The bishops of the Churches in the Americas, in their recent synod, asked believers to combat the sinful structures that cause misery for so many while "the rich becoming richer and the poor becoming poorer" (see the Synod of American Bishops' "Working Paper" 63).

Christians realize that humanity is redeemed from sin through the paschal mystery of Jesus Christ. Neither salvation nor sin is solely a personal affair. Humans are saved, not merely as individuals, but as members of a believing community. Salvation comes through community, in which believers acknowledge and serve the Lord of truth in holiness.

For Christians, the way of salvation is not separate from the cross. Christ's example of suffering leads followers through death into life (Rom 8:11). Christians have a need and duty to battle against evil through difficulties, even if need be, to the point of death. This battle with evil structures involves a raising of consciousness of the Christian community, so that the cross is situated at the center of history. Reflecting on the cruel suffering inflicted on Christ, the cross demands that society address those attitudes and practices that encourage any person to treat another contrary to dignity.

Structural/Social Sin

Preparation Page

Purpose: To examine consequences of structural/social sin. To celebrate reconciliation in an optional penance prayer service.

Basic Materials: name tags, newsprint, markers, percussion instrument, cloth, candle, Bibles, seasonal sign, matches, pens or pencils, masking tape, songbooks or words reproduced with permission

Additional Materials: mission magazines with pictures of the world's poor and colored paper or "The Stations of the Cross Posters," index cards, news stories or video with video player

Music: "God Revealed" and "Because We Are God's Chosen Ones" from *A Eucharistic People*; for the penance prayer service, "Healing Is Your Touch" from *A Remembering Heart*

Refreshments: Serve beverages only. Fast from solid foods or serve something made from rice as a reminder of those who have only a little rice to eat.

Getting Ready: Refer to "Preparation Checklist for Each Session" to set up the room, the prayer space, and refreshment items.

■ Choose an "Opening" option: From mission magazines, cut out pictures of the world's poor, mount on colored paper, and display on the walls, or display "The Stations of the Cross Posters" from Maryknoll World Publications (800-227-8523).

■ Plan to ask a volunteer to prepare Ephesians 5:6–17 for the beginning prayer.

■ Choose a "From Our Experience" option: For the news option, obtain newspaper sections and magazines. For the video options, obtain *The Challenge to End Hunger* from Food First (website: www.foodfirst.org; or call 510-654-4400), or *Banking on Life and Debt* from Maryknoll World Publications (800-227-8523), or choose another video that explores structural sin.

■ Plan to ask volunteers to prepare Jeremiah 6:13–16; Matthew 7:13–14; and Hosea 4:1–3 for the session.

■ Make copies of the "Voiceless Injustices" and "Beyond Charity into Justice" handouts found at the end of the session.

■ Decide which closing options will be used. Consider the time the penance prayer service will require, and adjust accordingly or offer it at another time.

■ For the "Penance Prayer Service" option: For sacramental penance with absolution, ask a priest to preside. Otherwise, ask a trained layperson to preside. Encourage the members to seek sacramental penance as convenient. Make a copy of the liturgical plan for the presider, and ask the person to prepare a homily/reflection. Ask four readers to prepare Obadiah 2–4; 13–15; James 5:1–6; Matthew 11:28, and the Examination of Conscience. Obtain songbooks or permission to copy words for songs.

■ For the Group Prayer option: Ask volunteers to prepare James 5:1–6 and Luke 16:19–31. Write the suggested petitions found in the prayer on paper slips and ask volunteers to say them during the prayer.

Strategy Hint: Draw on the resources of the parish and community. Invite a community member who works for social justice on the local level, or ask the pastor to address justice issues in the church. A recent immigrant can give insights into the difficulties people face in moving from another country. (Provide a translator if necessary.) Prepare a list of local names and phone numbers so participants can find more information on their own.

Structural/Social Sin

Session Plan Outline

Opening

Welcome. Greet members as they arrive, and hand out name tags. Invite them to walk through the picture display of the world's poor or the Maryknoll "The Stations of the Cross Posters."

Gathering Prayer. Strike an instrument to call members to the prayer space. Indicate the order of prayer and distribute the songbooks or singing aid.

Leader: We gather as Christians + united as a light of hope for those who are suffering. We reflect on Scripture as our source of inspiration and insight.

All: *Sing "God Revealed" from* A Eucharistic People.

Reader: *Proclaims Ephesians 5:6–17 and concludes with, "The word of the Lord."*

All: Thanks be to God.

Leader: Creator God, you have called us as Christians to be your light in the world. Help us to discern ways to counteract evil in our society and in the world, so your love may fully reign among people. Bless our efforts to understand your way. In the Spirit of Christ, our Lord.

All: Amen.

From Our Experience

Awareness of structural sin. Choose one of the options to introduce structural/social sin.

In the News Option. Divide the members into groups of four or five. Distribute a variety of newspaper news and entertainment sections and magazines. Ask the members to determine what sinful attitudes and values permeate and are promoted in the media. Ask for feedback to the large group. Together, conclude some major sins of the society (for example, indulgent overconsumption, sexism, violence, prejudice).

Structural Sin and Hunger Option. Show the video *The Challenge to End Hunger* from Food First to uncover some of the structural causes of hunger. After the video, ask the following questions and jot down highlights on newsprint:
- What are some of the causes of world hunger?
- What role does food aid play? How does it help? How does it perpetuate hunger?
- What kind of actions would help change the face of hunger?
- Is it a sin that so many of the world's poor are starving? If so, whose responsibility is this sin? Individuals? Governments? Corporations?

Alternate Video Option. Show *Banking on Life and Debt* or another video that depicts a social sin besides hunger, and adjust the above questions.

Scripture and Tradition

From Scripture. Explain in the following or similar words:

> **The realization of the social nature of sin was a given in biblical times. Our modern individualistic approach to sin and repentance has camouflaged sinful structures of which the ancients had a keen awareness. Scripture sheds light on social sin and inspires just action.**

In an open forum, ask the members what they heard by using the questions after each.

Have a reader proclaim Jeremiah 6:13–16.

- **What is the connection between peace and justice? What sins make peace impossible?**

Have a reader proclaim Matthew 7:13–14.

- **What are some of the structures in the world today that lead to the broad way of destruction? How does our call to conversion lead us to the narrow gate?**

Have a reader proclaim Hosea 4:1–3.

- **What are the consequences of social sin and unjust societal structures? What are the consequences for the environment?**

From Church Social Teaching: Social Sin and Social Justice. Divide into groups of five or six. Distribute the "Voiceless Injustices" handout and pencils. Assign each group two categories on the list, and ask them to identify any social sins related to these groups, what structural and attitudinal changes are needed, and at what level. Have them make suggestions about how these changes may be facilitated and report to the large group.

Break. Serve beverages. Fast from solid food, or offer rice cakes or a scoop of rice in a cup as a reminder of those who have little.

Called to Live Justly

Charity and Justice Option. (If this option is not used during the session, distribute the "Beyond Charity into Justice" handout for members to work through at home.) Divide the members into groups of four or five. Distribute the "Beyond Charity into Justice" handout. Have the groups read explanations of charity and justice and discuss the questions.

Together summarize the session. Distribute cards and pencils. Ask each person to write down one action they might take to change an unjust structure or attitude.

Penance Service Option: Forgiveness of Social Sins. Use this option in place of both "Called to Live Justly" and "Group Prayer." Refer to the "Penance Service: Forgiveness of Social Sins" at the end of this session as a guide. This service will offer an examination of conscience that may stimulate a desire for absolution. If a layperson or deacon presides during the reconciliation service, suggest that the members may seek sacramental penance for absolution with a priest as soon as it is convenient.

Group Prayer   If the "Penance Prayer Service" is not used, consider offering it at another time. Conclude with the following group prayer.

Leader's Call to Prayer: Let us gather around the prayer table to reflect on the insights we have shared. (*Indicate the order of prayer.*)

Leader: Lord God, Creator of a bountiful world, lead us in ways to truly help the poor and suffering. Help us understand our own prejudices and selfish ways. Grant us your grace and strengthen us by your word.

Reader 1: *Proclaims James 5:1–6 and concludes with, "The word of the Lord."*

All: Thanks be to God.

All: *Respond in song: "Because We Are God's Chosen Ones" from* A Eucharistic People.

Reader 2: *Reads from the Gospel of Luke.*

All: Glory to you, Lord.

Reader 2: *Proclaims Luke 16:19–31, ending with, "The Gospel of the Lord."*

All: Praise to you, Lord Jesus Christ.

Leader: Please respond to the following with, "Lord, guide us in your ways."

(*Members who were given prompts on slips of paper begin the petitions.*)

That we may discern the needs of the poor, responding both in charity and justice, we pray.

That we may be the light that instills in others a sense of justice, we pray.

That those oppressed by structural sins may experience the mercy of God at work in the world, we pray.

(*With a hand gesture, invite other petitions.*)

Glory to God in the highest, and to Jesus Christ, our redeemer, whose Spirit dwells among us. Enkindle in our hearts a love for all humanity, especially the poor and oppressed. Arouse in your faithful ones a hunger and thirst for social justice and mercy. Make us, O Lord, instruments of your peace in our souls, in our families, in our country, and in our world.

All: Amen.

Leader: Let us go forth to love and serve as we offer one another a sign of peace.

Voiceless Injustices

*I*n 1971, the Synod of Bishops identified the following types as voiceless victims of social injustices. They called on every sector of society, from the local to the global level, to address the need for structural change by taking on new tasks and duties. Consequently, much has been accomplished but much remains to be done.

Consider each of the following categories, and suggest what still needs to be done in the nation and world:

1. Migrant discrimination and lack of security:

2. Lower-level workers:

3. Refugees and those who suffer racial or ethnic persecution:

4. Those persecuted for their faith or are deprived of religious liberty:

5. Political prisoners and those who suffer from war crimes:

6. Those denied a right to life because of abortion, war, and capital punishment:

7. Those manipulated by the media and media rights:

8. Children and youth morally threatened by the media and those without an adequate education:

9. Families with insufficient social opportunities:

10. The abandoned, the sick, the elderly, and orphans:

This handout draws from the Synod of Bishops, "Voiceless Injustice," *Justice in the World (1971)*.

Charity and the call to justice are two ways of reacting to the needs of those who are suffering. Charity is necessary as an initial response to such problems as hunger and disease, but action on behalf of justice is necessary if oppression is to be eliminated. Justice, the process that ensures fair treatment of all by addressing structural and social sin,* is determined by the actions of people in society. The community, the nation, the world, and the structures within each level all either contribute to social sin or to just actions. Justice allows individuals to take control of their lives, so they no longer need to depend on charity.

Charity is temporary relief.

- With charity, there is never a question as to what needs to be done, such as the need to feed someone hungry.
- Normally, charity is a short-term solution to alleviate the problems after a disaster. Charity may be necessary as an initial response to an unjust situation, but it alone will only perpetuate abuses.
- Charity is never the permanent or ongoing solution.
- Charity does not impact social sin or address deep-rooted problems.
- Jesus acts in charity when he heals the woman with the hemorrhage (see Lk 8:43–48).

Indicate some situations in which charity is the necessary response:

1.

2.

3.

Justice calls for permanent changes.

- Social sins threaten human dignity and call for attitudinal and structural changes.
- Structures of social sin include attitudes, prejudices, laws, policies, and distorted values.
- The necessary response to social sin requires justice actions for long-term results.
- Because social sins are ingrained in a culture, several options for change are possible, and the best solution may be difficult to determine.
- Justice efforts—attacks on the structural causes of inequities—are often controversial.
- Such changes require organized plans and involve government and other institutions.
- Jesus acts in justice in opposing the misuse of the Temple (see Lk 19:45–46).

Identify some justice issues in which social sins require a change in structures or attitudes:

1.

2.

3.

Structural and social sin are interrelated. Structural sins are perpetuated by policies and regulations. Social sins are attitudes and prejudices that foster unjust policies and behaviors.

Penance Prayer Service: Forgiveness of Social Sins

Opening

(*All stand.*)

All: *Sing "Healing Is Your Touch" from* A Remembering Heart.

Presider's Greeting: May God open our hearts to know the ways of peace. May grace and wisdom help us overcome our sinful ways so that justice will reign. Glory to God forever.

All: Amen.

Opening Prayer: O God, send your Spirit to strengthen our resolve. Turn us away from sin, and give us the courage to stand against sinful structures. Make us willing to sacrifice ways of luxury and resist the temptations of our time. We ask this through Christ our Lord.

All: Amen.

(*All be seated.*)

Scripture

First Reading: *Reader proclaims Obadiah 2-4; 13-15.*

All: *Sing "Because We Are God's Chosen Ones" from* A Eucharistic People.

Second Reading: *Reader proclaims James 5:1-6.*

(*All stand.*)

Gospel Acclamation: *Reader proclaims Matthew 11:28.*

Gospel: *Presider proclaims Matthew 25:31-46.*

(*All be seated.*)

Homily/Reflection Notes:

- In Hebrew Scriptures, sin is always associated with a people as a whole. The tendency to sin is carried within the culture, and the whole nation is called to repentance.

- What are the prides given to us by the culture that drive us to seek selfish goals, and how do they deceive? What deeds as a nation do we need to fear coming back on us?

- How does God bring righteousness to the oppressed?

- How can we be delivered from sin as a people?

- Considering the poverty in the world, are we among the "rich"? What does our society encourage us to think of as valuable that are susceptible to rot and corrosion? Who suffers so we can enjoy luxuries? What might we be doing instead of "fattening our hearts"?

**Examination
of Conscience**

Reader: *Ask the participants to reflect during the following litany of questions. Read each question slowly and pause after each.*

When have I failed to be a leaven for justice at home? In my school or workplace?

When have I accepted jokes and everyday conversations that demean others in some way?

What civic responsibilities have I neglected?

What temptations toward sin do I experience in my own social group?

When do I put my individualistic desires before the betterment of society?

What am I afraid to stand against that should be changed in the community, parish, or the world?

What possessions do I have to enhance my feeling of social status?

What values do I perpetuate that cause some sort of injustice to others?

What are my prejudices?

What sinfulness that is encouraged by media do I enjoy?

Have I failed to exercise my right to vote responsibly?

Do I write to the legislators to encourage just decisions?

What attitudes do I still need to renounce?

Presider: Take a moment of silence to reflect on social ills. Ask yourself what more you could do to help change attitudes and policies. Examine what you need to change in yourself.

(All stand.)

**Prayers
of Repentance**

Presider: Let us say together an act of confession. "I confess to almighty God ..."

May our merciful God forgive each of us for the part we play in perpetuating social sin. May our community, our parish, and our nation be purged of harmful ways. May we be shown our faults in the light of day so they may be changed. Let us ask for God's mercy by responding, "Lord, have mercy," to each of the following petitions:

Christ our Savior, help us follow you as a model of inclusive love.

All: Lord, have mercy.

Presider: You see our sinful attitudes and forgive those who are truly sorry.

All: Lord, have mercy.

Presider: You call us to repentance and new life.

All: Lord, have mercy.

Presider: For those who suffer from war and international debt.

All: Lord, have mercy.

Presider: For all the oppressed, especially women and children.

All: Lord, have mercy.

Presider: Renew your love in our hearts, and help us welcome all.

All: Lord, have mercy.

Presider: Let us pray together for forgiveness and resistance to temptations of society in the words Jesus gave us.

All: Our Father ...

Presider: God of mercy, you know our evil ways. Only you can free us from sin. Renew your Spirit within us so that we can live as your people. Be with those who have been hurt by our neglectful ways. We ask this through Christ our Lord.

All: Amen.

Concluding Prayer

Presider: Wonderful and merciful God, you show your mercy and forgive our sins. Help us discern evil structures. Continue to transform us so your love and care may be felt by all. We ask this through Christ our Lord.

All: Amen.

Presider: May the Lord bless us all, the Father, and the Son, and the Holy Spirit.

All: Amen.

(*Option:* If a priest is available, consider offering sacramental penance with absolution.)

The Reign of God

Background Notes

The reign of God, the central theme of the ministry of Jesus of Nazareth, revealed in Christ's word, works, and presence (Mk 1:15; Mt 4:17, 12:28; Lk 11:20), is proclaimed by the living Church. The paschal mystery, Jesus' life, death, and resurrection, inaugurates God's dominion of love. This new age of love and justice is central to the mission of Jesus.

Jesus inaugurated the reign of God by challenging systems. He refused to conform to the social, political, and religious standards of his day. He broke the religious laws and ate with the unclean. Jesus demanded a total commitment of disciples, just as he surrendered himself totally to God's love. Through Jesus' total self-giving, God has reigned victoriously over death, and the dominion of justice has become available for humanity.

As an evangelizer, Jesus first has proclaimed a new era whereby God reigns in the hearts of followers; and this is so important that, by comparison, everything else becomes the rest and given in addition (Mt 6:33). Only the reign of God, therefore, is absolute and makes everything else relative to it (see *On Evangelization in the Modern World* 8). An understanding, then, of the depth and dimension of God's dominion is fundamental to Christian commitment, from which the call to justice emerges from a desire to live according to Christ's Spirit.

Scripture scholarship tells us the expression "the *basileia* of God is at hand" (Mk 1:15) refers to a good and benevolent rule (see Smith 112–13). Because the reign of God is a just rule for everyone, believers are inspired to make efforts that alleviate human misery in the world. In reigning over evil, God exercises dominion over oppression. Jesus, prophet of the reign of God, summons believers to respond to the saving act of love by promoting the Spirit of peace, justice, freedom, and life. Jesus gives us the Spirit to guide believers to live as members of the new dominion.

The Spirit-guided domain is neither a place nor a hereafter experience but a promise of redemption. Believers who live in this new realm are called to a change of heart so that love becomes the central principle of life. This call to conversion, not a one-time act, is a lifelong process. Fidelity to the Spirit of truth and justice calls followers to make ever-deeper decisions in light of God's justice.

The miracles of Jesus are a sign of the new age proclaimed. The wonderous deeds worked by Jesus indicate an era of hope for the hopeless (Mt 11:5; Lk 7:22). Through cures and exorcisms, Jesus freed people who were bound to ailments and possession so that they could have new life. Through Jesus, persons are restored to become disciples themselves at the service of others. Disciples, after the example of Jesus, promote a transformation of a world of sin into a world of human unity and celebrate God's victorious dominion over sin and death in sacramental worship (see McKenna).

Pope John Paul II reminds us of the impact the eternal domain has on earthly time. The kingdom of God, although not *of* the world, brings Gospel values *to* the world (see *On the Hundredth Anniversary* 25).

Believers are sanctified to bring the light, truth, and courage of God's reign to human realities. The reign of God, a transcendental mystery, buds within historical, worldly activities. Jesus, in proclaiming the reign of God (Mk 1:15; Lk 17:20–21), called believers to help bring the reality to fulfillment. God's realm impacts the world when hearers respond to the Good News with actions that conform to justice. Since the reign of God on earth is truly present yet not complete, Christians live with a "here, but not fully yet" tension in their struggles for a more just world.

The daily decisions of all believers should serve God's domain. By calling on the Spirit, Christians gain help to distinguish between those actions that

support God's reign and actions that are only for worldly satisfaction. We, as followers of Christ, need to take assertive action and, also, be ready for suffering, self-denial, forgiveness of enemies, or possibly the giving of our own lives. As Jesus emptied himself to the point of death (Phil 2:6–8) and poured out his blood for the good of all (Lk 22:20), followers also must be ready for such difficulties and sacrifices (1 Pt 2:20–23). Christians discover along with Jesus the power of sin against those with kingdom values. The faithful face many challenges to bring God's liberating hope and justice to a troubled world (see *Lumen Gentium* in Abbott's *The Documents of Vatican II* 36). In Christian witness, we evaluate our daily occupations and make the necessary changes so that all work will spread the glory of God.

The church, while not equated to the kingdom, is the earthly, Spirit-guided agent through which Jesus' initial work of proclaiming God's loving reign is continued. The people of God, disregarding earthly distinctions that cause division, respond to the needs of the world community without conforming to them. Through word and deed, Jesus has showed us the possibilities of transforming the world when we open ourselves to the will of God who reigns triumphant. As the proclaimer of God's reign, the church's mission is to serve so that all human life is transformed according to Divine Justice.

The Reign of God

Preparation Page

Purpose: To probe the relationship of the church in the modern world and the reign of God.

Basic Materials: name tags, newsprint, markers, percussion instrument, cloth, candle, Bibles, seasonal sign, matches, pens or pencils, masking tape, songbooks or words reproduced with permission

Additional Materials: index cards, a variety of expressive materials or Beatitude posters

Music: "Everybody Get Ready" from *A Eucharistic People*

Refreshments: Plan refreshments that celebrate belonging (for example, bread, wine, crackers, cheese).

Getting Ready: Refer to "Preparation Checklist for Each Session" to set up the room, the prayer space, and refreshment items.

■ Choose an Opening option: **For the creative option:** Set out expressive media: clay, paints, simple musical instruments and score sheets, graph paper, building blocks, simple costumes, soap and carving tools, and clean-up supplies. Display the creative materials around the room with work space. **For the Beatitudes option:** Obtain Beatitudes posters with the Study Guide from Maryknoll World Productions (800-227-8523). Display them around the room.

■ Plan to ask volunteers to prepare to proclaim Luke 17:20–21 and Matthew 24:4,11–14 during prayers.

■ Make copies of the "What Does the Church Say about the Kingdom of God?" handout found at the end of the session.

■ Make copies of the "Evaluation Form" handout or create one.

Strategy Hint: Have reasonable expectations. Keep in mind that conversion is an ongoing process. The goal of justice awareness catechesis is not to solve the myriad of world problems, but to help believers act more justly in their daily lives. The process may lead to special interest action groups. Some possible themes are family and children concerns, the environment, media influences, or world issues.

Evaluation Process: Evaluation is the final step that completes any catechesis and helps the facilitator plan the next process. The review strengthens the participants' assimilation of the concepts, while affirming and giving insights to the leader. The catechist may ask for feedback in a variety of ways, but a form that allows written input from participants is usually the easiest. An "Evaluation Form" is found at the end of this session, or design a tool using open-ended or multiple-choice questions or a ranking system. While open-ended questions allow for personal comments, other tools may be easier to answer and compute. Participants may fill out a form before leaving or submit it by fax, e-mail, or dropping it at the parish office by a given deadline.

The evaluation tool will help the facilitator assess the effectiveness of the catechesis. It will help the leader determine if the process is merely academic or actually sensitizes members and calls them to further action. The evaluation process reaffirms the participants' commitment to support one another as successful agents of change in the parish and community.

The director assures further catechesis that may be indicated by the participants. See the appendix for materials. The director may also help form support groups to work and pray together for ongoing conversion within the parish.

The Reign of God

Session Plan Outline

Opening

Welcome. Greet members as they arrive. Invite them to put on a name tag.

Creative Option. Offer the creative materials, and ask the members to choose a medium and depict the kingdom of God. Tell them they may work together or independently. Allow twenty minutes.

Beatitudes Option. Encourage the participants to walk through the Beatitude poster display.

Gathering Prayer. After sufficient time, call the members to prayer by striking an instrument. Indicate the order of prayer.

All: *Sing "Everybody Get Ready" from* **A Eucharistic People.**

Leader: **We gather as servants to the reign of God to carry forth the mission of Jesus.**

Reader: *Proclaims Luke 17:20–21 and concludes with, "The Gospel of the Lord."*

All: **Praise to you Lord, Jesus Christ.**

Leader: **Creator God, you call us as Christians to continue the mission of actuating the kingdom. Help us discern ways to act so that justice and salvation will be realized for an ever-growing number of people. Bless our efforts to understand your way. In the Spirit of Christ, our Lord,**

All: **Amen.**

From Our Experience

Kingdom Renditions Option. Encourage all who would like to share their versions of the kingdom of God to do so. Affirm each contribution.

Beatitudes Option. Tell about the "Blessed are the poor in spirit" poster. Adapt the Study Guide that is part of the poster package for adults, and ask the discussion questions. (Offer the Study Guide during the break to members who want to learn about the other posters.)

Scripture and Tradition

In the following or similar words, recall the principle of solidarity:

> **When human beings live in love and service to one another, liberation, justice, and peace thrive. Solidarity is the attitude of people who identify with the reign of God that is revealed through the paschal mystery, the life, death, and resurrection of Jesus Christ. Scripture helps us identify characteristics of God's domain.**

From Scripture: The Reign of God. Divide the members into groups of four or five to determine what characteristic of the kingdom is revealed in each pair of the following passages. Write the Scripture pairs on newsprint and assign various passages to the groups.

- Matthew 6:33, Matthew 13:46 (The kingdom is more important than anything else.)
- Mark 1:15, Matthew 10:7 (The kingdom is at hand.)
- Mark 1:15, Matthew 3:2 (The kingdom requires repentance.)
- Matthew 4:23, Matthew 11:12 (The kingdom is for those who suffer.)
- Luke 12:32, Luke 22:29–30 (The kingdom is a gift.)
- Matthew 19:15, Mark 10:14 (The kingdom is for those who are like children.)
- Luke 22:28–29, Acts 14:22 (The kingdom comes after trials and hardships.)

As members share insights, make notes on newsprint. If they did the creative option, ask them how these images compare with the exercise they did in the opening segment.

From Catholic Teaching: The Kingdom. Distribute the "What Does the Church Say about the Kingdom of God?" handout. Divide into groups of four or five. Ask them to read the excerpts and discuss the questions. (*Option:* Assign each group one section to discuss.) In the large group, share the highlights of the small-group discussions. Conclude that the church carries on Jesus' mission of actuating the kingdom. This work demands a commitment to justice and solidarity, as hope is brought to the hopeless.

Break. Serve refreshments that help celebrate God's reign on earth.

Called to Live Justly

Discuss how the reality of the reign of God impacts everyone as individuals and as members of a parish community. Help the members form a commitment to the mission of Jesus. After each question, ask two or three members to offer a suggestion. This activity is not intended to be a discussion but to encourage the participants to live by justice principles.

- Jesus ate with sinners and society's outcasts. What action is indicated for us?
- The kingdom exists in the midst of the world. How do we, in our daily lives, carry out the mission of Jesus to combat injustices and to defend the oppressed?
- How does our parish live kingdom values by
  welcoming immigrants and sharing multicultural gifts?
  helping migrants and the homeless meet their needs?
  fully including members of different income, sex, age, race, or social status in all aspects of parish life?

Conclude with the following:

- **While the realization of all the wrongs in the world can be disheartening, the reality of the reign of God brings hope and courage to believers.**

- Good intentions are not enough; justice principles must be put into practice and reinforced by the community.

Option: Together, choose one issue for the group members to work on. This may be a continuation of efforts began in a previous session. Set a date for a committee meeting for those who would like to continue meeting and supporting one another.

Distribute cards, and have members write a commitment to the chosen project or one of their own intentions.

Group Prayer

Ask the members to hold their commitment cards and gather in a circle around the prayer table. Indicate the order of prayer.

Leader: Lord God, Just Ruler, help us in our ongoing conversion. Make us servants of your domain. Help us take action for the sake of justice, so your will may be done on earth.

Reader: *Proclaims Matthew 24:4,11–14 and concludes with, "The Gospel of the Lord."*

All: Praise to you Lord, Jesus Christ.

Leader: Please respond to the following with, "Thy will be done."

That the Lord will strengthen us in our ongoing conversion, we pray.

That we may have wisdom to discern injustices, we pray.

That we may have courage to seek changes that lead to liberation, we pray.

That we have perseverance in the commitment we hold written in our hands, we pray.

With a hand motion, invite other petitions.

Glory to God in the highest, and to Jesus Christ, our redeemer, whose Spirit dwells among us. Enkindle in our hearts a love for all humanity, especially the poor and oppressed. Arouse in your faithful ones a hunger and thirst for social justice and mercy. Make us, O Lord, instruments of your peace in our souls, in our families, in our country, and in our world.

All: Amen.

Leader: Let us go forth to love and serve as we sing together.

All: *Sing "Everybody Get Ready" from* A Eucharistic People.

Distribute the "Evaluation Form" and pens. Ask them to fill out the form.

Thank everyone for attending the sessions.

What Does the Church Say about the Kingdom of God?

Consider the following summaries from ecclesial documents. Discuss church teachings about the reign of God.

From *Gaudium et Spes* (*Pastoral Constitution on the Church in the Modern World*) 45, in *The Documents of Vatican II* (Abbott):

> The Church, while helping the world and receiving benefits from it, has a single intention: that God's kingdom may come for the salvation of the whole human race.

How does the church help the world so that salvation through the kingdom can come?

From *Evangelii Nuntiandi* (*On Evangelization in the Modern World*) 3–8:

> Christ first of all proclaims the kingdom of God; everything else becomes 'the rest,' (Mt 6:33). Only the kingdom is Absolute and makes everything else relative. The kingdom brings salvation, which is liberation from everything that oppresses. This kingdom and this salvation, through a total interior renewal which the Gospel calls metanoia, belong to the violent. Conversion is realized through toil and suffering, through a life lived according to the Gospel, through abnegation and the cross, through the spirit of the beatitudes.

What happens to the "violent" who come to gain salvation through the kingdom? How does the concept of liberation relate to God's reign of justice?

From *Sharing the Light of Faith* 30 and 53:

> The Church continues the mission of Jesus, prophet, priest, and servant king, which is to bring about God's kingdom. He confronted the sinful, dehumanizing forces that alienate people from God and other human beings.

What dehumanizing forces must we confront today in order to continue the mission of Jesus?

From *Catechism of the Catholic Church* 544 and 2820:

> Jesus makes active love toward the poor of every kind the condition for entering his kingdom. The Christian responsibility is to distinguish between the growth of the reign of God and the progress of society.

When does the progress of society aid the kingdom? How is progress sometimes an impediment to it?

Mark a slash on the scale after each sentence (mark 1 for lowest and 10 for highest) to reflect your opinion of the justice catechesis process. Thank you for your participation.

1. The sessions gave me insight into the Scriptural base for church social teaching. **1 2 3 4 5 6 7 8 9 10**

   Comments:

2. The sessions gave me a better understanding of the church documents that promulgate church social teaching. **1 2 3 4 5 6 7 8 9 10**

   Comments:

3. I have a better awareness of justice issues in my daily activities and the world situation. **1 2 3 4 5 6 7 8 9 10**

   Comments:

4. The time for discussion was helpful. **1 2 3 4 5 6 7 8 9 10**

   Comments:

5. I would attend other catechetical programs regarding justice issues.
   1 2 3 4 5 6 7 8 9 10

   Comments:

6. What do you believe was good about the process?

7. How would you improve the process?

8. How can we, as a parish, reinforce one another's justice efforts?

Resource Appendix

A parish profile is a helpful tool to adapt any catechesis to local needs. The insights gained from the profile data are helpful to design a meaningful catechesis that meets the needs of the participants. A parish may keep a basic profile available on file for general planning.

A profile of the parish community is particularly useful for an effective justice catechesis. For instance, the process will take a different form for parishes with a high immigrant population, those located in high crime areas, others with an active charity ministry, and so on. To develop a profile, draw on parish records, school district information, the local newspaper's statistics, and city demographics to compile as much of the following information as possible.

Developing the Profile

Use the data sheet to identify parish needs.

1. Identify ethnic groups whose interests and needs may differ.

2. Are there specific immigrant needs, such as language or citizenship classes?

3. What kind of ministry is needed for the divorced and widowed?

4. What kind of support is needed for parents and their school-age children?

5. Is there high crime or a high school dropout rate? If so, how can the parish intervene?

6. Can the parish serve as an agent for government programs, such as food distribution or citizenship programs?

7. What are the particular needs of senior citizens in the parish?

8. Do the youth programs meet real needs?

9. Does the parish need to foster small-based communities for diverse neighborhoods?

10. Do the parish liturgies represent a balance that respects diversity while also providing for unity?

11. Is there a gender imbalance, such as an abundance of widows or single males? If so, what are their needs?

12. Reflect on the life signs to identify the top five needs of your parish.

Keep the parish profile available for all parish catechesis. The life signs that emerge will shape all ministry in the parish.

In addition to the parish profile, a participants' profile will provide the basis for each specific catechetical ministry and process. These more-specific profiles can be drawn from specifically designed registration forms for each program. Pertinent questions can indicate life signs.

Parish Profile Data Worksheet

Age:		Number
0–4	F	_____
	M	_____
5–12	F	_____
	M	_____
13–18	F	_____
	M	_____
19–25	F	_____
	M	_____
26–50	F	_____
	M	_____
50–70	F	_____
	M	_____
> 70	F	_____
	M	_____

Family Status:

Adult/Single	_____
Married/Raising Children	_____
Married Couple	_____
Single/Parent	_____
Widow/Widower	_____
Divorced	_____

Ethnicity:

Hispanic	_____
Afro-American	_____
Native American	_____
Asian	_____
Other:	
_____	_____
_____	_____

Immigrant Status:	Number
U.S. Citizen	_____
Documented	_____
Undocumented (est.)	_____

Distinctive Neighborhoods:

_____

_____

Household Income:

< $25,000	_____
$25–50,000	_____
$50–100,000	_____
> $100,000	_____

Education (Head of Household):

< 12 years	_____
High School	_____
College	_____
Post Graduate	_____

Major Employers:

_____

_____

Charity/Justice Groups:

_____

_____

Other Factors:

_____

_____

_____

_____

Organizations Dedicated to Justice

The church is blessed with numerous organizations dedicated to the goal of seeking dignity for all people. For a wealth of brochures, publications, and project ideas, contact some of the groups listed below:

Bread for the World, 1100 Wayne Ave., Suite 1000, Silver Spring, MD 20910 (phone: 301-608-2400; fax: 301-608-2401). A nonpartisan Christian movement dedicated to ending hunger through legislation. Publishes an Offering of Letters kit that includes everything needed to organize a letter-writing campaign for your church or group.

Campaign for Human Development: The Catholic Church Working to End Poverty and Injustice in America, United States Catholic Conference, 3211 Fourth St., NE, Washington, D.C. 20017-1194 (800-946-4CHD). Supports self-help projects so that poor people can take control of their lives, and works to change conditions that cause poverty. Publishes an abundance of materials, including lesson plans, and will help set up a Social Concerns Committee in your parish. Request a resource catalog.

Catholic Relief Services — 209 West Fayette St., Baltimore, MD 21201-3443 (410-625-2220). Gives active witness to the mandate of Jesus Christ to respond to human needs. Alleviates immediate needs, and supports self-help programs. Will provide an abundance of materials for awareness. Ask for "Work of Human Hands" catalog for beautiful and reasonably priced gifts from around the world. Supports low-income craftspeople, your parish projects, and the CRS program in your diocese (800-685-7572).

Columban Fathers and Sisters, Mission Awareness Resources, Mission Education Office, St. Columbans, NE 68056 (402-291-1920). Missionaries around the world help groups attack their sources of poverty and see true hope in the message of Jesus. An awareness program includes lesson plans, videos, posters, and handouts for various age levels, through free loan or purchase.

Concern/America, 2024 N. Broadway 104, P.O. Box 1790, Santa Ana, CA 92702 (800-CONCERN). An international development and refugee aid organization. Trains members of poor communities to become victors instead of victims. Provides preventative health care and technology, and enables the organization of cooperatives to alleviate underemployment. Depends on parishes to promote craft sales and sponsorship. Will send brochures or a guest speaker.

Maryknoll World Productions, P.O. Box 308, Maryknoll, NY 10545-0308 (800-227-8523). Witnesses to the word of God in thirty-eight countries help people to alter the structures that create poverty. Depends on Partners in Mission from parishes. Makes available an abundance of videos, posters, magazines, and speakers.

The National Catholic Reporter Publishing Company, 115 E. Armour Blvd., Kansas City, MO 64111. Addresses the need to further proclaim the church's social teachings, so the lives of Catholics are influenced. Publishes NCR, parish resources and newsletters.

Orbis Books, Dept. 897, Box 302, Maryknoll, NY 10545-0302 (800-258-5838). Committed to the preferential option for the poor. Publishes books, videos, and journals.

Parish Resources from the U.S. Catholic Bishops, Publishing Services, United States Catholic Conference, 3211 Fourth Street, NE, Washington, D.C. 20017-1194 (800-235-8722). Publishes a variety of social justice documents. Especially good for materials to use with special interest action groups. Some complete programs are available, such as "A Catholic Campaign for Children and Families," understanding immigrants, and environmental justice programs that include resource and background information, study guides, liturgical helps, handouts, clip art, and videos.

Salt of the Earth, Claretian Publications (http//www.claret.org/~salt/). Now the on-line resource for social justice (previously a print journal). A means to introduce the long tradition of Catholic social teaching and mission to the parish community. Provides social justice news, legislation, statistics, links, idea exchanges, archives, and a help zone. Catholic Wisdom is an inexpensive series of booklets that is designed to explain the church's position and wisdom on today's social issues. Attractive and easy-to-understand information on immigration, abortion, the death penalty, environment, assisted suicide, and welfare reform. Order on-line or call 800-328-6515.

Ongoing Justice Catechesis

Easy-to-Use Resources

A variety of booklets and special programs are available from various sources for ongoing catechesis. The following are some short publications that members may read and discuss in small faith communities or other group formats. They were chosen for their brevity, accessibility, affordability, and timely publication.

- *The Cries of the Poor Are Still with Us: 25 Years of Working to Empower the Poor* (fifteen-page booklet available from USCC, 800-235-8722)

Discussion Questions

1. What do the signs of the times indicate about poverty in the United States? What facts or impressions can you add from your knowledge?

2. What economic, political, and educational factors have affected the trend toward inequality?

3. How are changes made in structures that create poverty?

4. Why is there hope?

5. What is the tension between the Christian mission and contemporary society?

6. What is the scriptural basis for concern for the poor?

7. What "social sin" can you name? What empowerment needs to occur?

8. What can we do in our parish/community to revive a commitment to the common good?

9. What are some unpopular issues that we need to speak out about to effect better solidarity?

10. Develop a prayer service on the theme "Committed to Making Hope a Reality."

- *Catechism of the Catholic Church* (Human Dignity, 1700–1748; Social Justice, 1897–1948, and the Kingdom of God, 2816–2820)

Discussion Questions

1. How is the dignity of the human person connected to the divine image?

2. How does the concept of Beatitude relate to the kingdom?

3. How is dignity related to freedom?

4. What conditions are necessary for true freedom?

5. Under what condition is an authority legitimate?

6. What are requirements for the common good?

7. How is social justice ensured?

8. What are sinful inequalities?

9. How is solidarity manifested?

10. What is the relationship between the growth of the reign of God and the progress of the society?

- *The Harvest of Justice Is Sown in Peace: A Reflection of the National Conference of Bishops on the Tenth Anniversary of the Challenge of Peace* (twenty-one pages, available from USCC, 800-235-8722)

Discussion Questions

1. What are two dimensions in the process of conversion to the God of peace?

2. What peaceable virtues do we need to cultivate?

3. Explain the statement, "Peace does not consist merely in the absence of war."

4. What are three major criteria for the Church's vision of a peaceful world?

5. What is the real potential power for nonviolent strategies?

6. What are the major components of the just-war tradition?

7. How do we develop an informed conscience for peace?

8. What five areas deserve special attention on the agenda for peacemaking?

9. Select one area, and develop a plan of action for your parish group.

10. Create a "Rite of Commitment" prayer service on the theme "Blessed Are the Peacemakers."

Other Suggestions for Ongoing Justice Catechesis

The United States Catholic Conference has numerous easy-to-use booklets with self-contained discussion questions and action ideas (800-235-8722). Materials such as the following are available in English and Spanish for use with parish groups:

- *Called to Global Solidarity: International Challenges for U.S. Parishes* (forty-two pages)
- *A Decade after* Economic Justice for All: *Continuing Principles, Changing Context, and New Challenges* (seventeen pages)
- *Communities of Salt and Light: Reflections on the Social Mission of the Parish* (eighteen pages; Parish Resource Manual and video also available)
- *Putting Children and Families First: A Challenge for Our Church, Nation, and World* (eighteen pages; Parish Resource Manual and video also available)

Suggested Readings and Music

Annotated Booklist

Baum, Gregory. *Religion and Alienation: A Theological Reading of Sociology*. New York: Paulist Press, 1975. A foundational work for understanding the nature of social sin.

Crosby, Michael H. *Spirituality of the Beatitudes: Matthew's Challenge for First World Christians*. Maryknoll, N.Y.: Orbis Books, 1981. 15th printing, October 1996. The number of printings attests to the usefulness of this resource. An intimate insight combining Scripture, modern Catholic social teaching, and story with scriptural and topical indices. Brings sensitivity to today's issues in light of the Gospel. A true integration of religious experience and social concern.

Henriot, Peter J., Edward P. DeBerri, and Michael J. Schultheis. *Catholic Social Teaching, Our Best Kept Secret: Centenary Edition*. Maryknoll, N.Y.: Orbis Books, 1992. Here is a century's worth of social justice wisdom to assist the Christian community in linking faith and justice. Presents an overview of the history of the church's social teaching, outlines important documents, and provides study guides and other information. Ideal for group study.

Lewis, Barbara A. *The Kid's Guide to Social Action: How to Solve the Problems You Choose—And Turn Creative Thinking into Positive Action*. Minneapolis: Free Spirit Publishing, 1991. This resource guide for learning political action skills is designed for teaching children but is a valuable resource for anyone who wants to make a difference. Includes skills, resources, and tools.

McKenna, Megan. *Rites of Justice: The Sacraments and Liturgy As Ethical Imperatives*. Maryknoll, N.Y.: Orbis Books, 1997. Packed with wonderful stories that enliven issues of justice and connect sacrament to life ethic through the person of Jesus Christ. Recognizes the difficulties in the call to do justice, love tenderly, and walk humbly with God. Includes a complete ritual (mini-retreat) to look at what issues of belief mean to believers in community practically and ethically. A story treasury.

O'Brien, David, and Thomas Shannon, eds. *Catholic Social Thought: The Documentary Heritage*. Maryknoll, N.Y.: Orbis Books, 1992. Comprehensive collection of major social documents, including encyclicals and pastoral letters of U.S. bishops. Includes introductions and an index.

Smith, Francis. *The God Question: A Catholic Approach*. New York: Paulist Press, 1988. Examines the mission of Jesus and the reign of justice he inaugurated.

United States Catholic Conference. *A Century of Social Teaching: A Common Heritage, A Continuing Challenge*. Washington, D.C.: Office for Publishing and Promotion Services, 1990. This twelve-page booklet for group introduction into the church's social teachings provides definitions of basic themes.

Articles from *Origins*: *CNS Documentary Services*

Origins: CNS Documentary Services, sponsored by the NCCB, publishes current ecclesial statements. For back issues: 202-541-3284; cnsinfo@aol.com; www.catholicnews.com. The following refer to issues regarding Catholic social teaching.

Archbishop Charles Chaput. "The Church and the Death Penalty." *Origins* 27, no. 6 (June 26, 1997).

Euart, Sharon. "Ten Years after the Pastoral on the Economy." *Origins* 26, no. 23 (November 21, 1996). Sharon Euart challenges how "the least among us" are faring. Vol.26, #23, November 21,1996.

Flynn, Raymond. "The Political Impact of Our Moral Choices." *Origins* 27, no. 6 (June 26, 1997).

George, Cardinal Francis. "How Globalization Challenges the Church's Mission." *Origins* 29, no. 27 (December 16, 1999).

John Paul II. "The Necessity of Jobs, the Meaning of Work." *Origins* 27, no. 6 (June 26, 1997).

———. "Toward a Balanced, Well-Regulated World Market." *Origins* 27, no. 3 (June 5, 1997). John Paul II's concern for the globalization of the economy.

Langan, John. "Issues in Catholic Social Thought." *Origins* 30, no. 3 (June 1, 2000).

Pontifical Council "Cor Unum." "World Hunger: A Challenge for All: Development in Solidarity." *Origins* 26, no. 21 (November 7, 1996).

U.S. Catholic Bishops. "A Catholic Framework for Economic Life." *Origins* 26, no.23 (November 21, 1996). Points for reflection, judgment, and actions.

———. "Sharing Catholic Social Teaching: Challenges and Directions." *Origins* 28, no. 7 (July 2, 1998).

Papal Documents

John XXIII. *Mater et Magistra: Christianity and Social Progress*. Washington, D.C.: National Catholic Welfare Conference, 1961.

———. *Pacem in Terris: Peace on Earth*. Washington, D.C.: National Catholic Welfare Conference, 1963.

John Paul II. *Centesimus Annus: On the Hundredth Anniversary of* Rerum Novarum. Washington, D.C.: United States Catholic Conference, 1991.

———. *Respect for Human Rights: The Secret of True Peace*. Washington, D.C.: United States Catholic Conference, 1999.

———. *Sollicitudo Rei Socialis: On Social Concern*. Washington, D.C.: United States Catholic Conference, 1987.

———. *Tertio Millennio Adveniente: On the Coming of the Third Millennium*. Washington, D.C.: United States Catholic Conference, 1994.

———. *The Ecological Crisis: A Common Responsibility*. Washington, D.C.: United States Catholic Conference, 1990.

Leo XIII. *Rerum Novarum: On the Condition of Workers*. Washington, D.C.: United States Catholic Conference, 1891.

Paul VI. *Octogesima Adveniens: A Call to Action: Apostolic Letter on the Eightieth Anniversary of* Rerum Novarum. Washington, D.C.: United States Catholic Conference, 1971.

———. *Evangelii Nuntiandi: On Evangelization in the Modern World*. Washington, D.C.: United States Catholic Conference, 1975.

———. *Populorum Progressio: On the Development of Peoples*. Washington, D.C.: United States Catholic Conference, 1967.

Pius XI. *Quadgragesimo Anno: After Forty Years*. Washington, D.C.: United States Catholic Conference, 1931.

Compiled Church Teachings

Abbott, Walter M., ed. *The Documents of Vatican II*. New York: The American Press, 1966. Includes *Guadium et Spes* and *Lumen Gentium*.

Libreria Editrice Vaticana. *Catechism of the Catholic Church*. 2nd ed. Washington, D.C.: United States Catholic Conference, 1997.

From the Bishops

Administrative Board of the United States Catholic Conference. *A Jubilee Call for Debt Forgiveness*. Washington, D.C.: United States Catholic Conference, 1999.

———. *Faithful Citizenship: Civic Responsibility for a New Millennium*. Washington, D.C.: United States Catholic Conference, 1999.

General Secretariat of the Synod of Bishops and the Pre-Synod Council. "Special Synod for America: The Working Paper." *Origins* 27, no. 13 (September 11, 1997).

International Theological Commission. *Propositions on the Dignity and Rights of the Human Person*. Washington, D.C.: United States Catholic Conference, 1986.

National Conference of Catholic Bishops. *Called to Global Solidarity: International Challenges for U.S. Parishes*. Washington, D.C.: United States Catholic Conference Office for Publishing and Promotion Services, 1997.

———. *Communities of Salt and Light: Reflections on the Social Mission of the Parish*. Washington, D.C.: United States Catholic Conference Office for Publishing and Promotion Services, 1993.

———. *The Harvest of Justice Is Sown in Peace: A Reflection of the National Conference of Bishops on the Tenth Anniversary of the Challenge of Peace*. Washington, D.C.: United States Catholic Conference Office for Publishing and Promotion Services, 1993.

———. *In All Things Charity: A Pastoral Challenge for the New Millennium*. Washington, D.C.: United States Catholic Conference, 1999.

———. *Sharing the Light of Faith: National Catechetical Directory for Catholics of the United States*. Washington, D.C.: United States Catholic Conference, 1979.

———. *Stewardship: A Disciple's Response*. Washington, D.C.: United States Catholic Conference, 1993.

National Conference of Catholic Bishops Committee on Migration. *From Newcomers to Citizens: All Come Bearing Gifts*. Washington, D.C.: United States Catholic Conference, 1999.

National Conference of Catholic Bishops on the Tenth Anniversary of the Economic Pastoral. *A Decade after* Economic Justice for All: *Continuing Principles, Changing Context, and New Challenges*. Washington, D.C.: United States Catholic Conference Office for Publishing and Promotion Services, 1995.

Synod of Bishops. *Justice in the World (1971)*. In *Catholic Social Thought: The Documentary Heritage,* edited by David O'Brien and Thomas Shannon. Maryknoll, N.Y.: Orbis Books, 1992.

United States Catholic Bishops. *The Cries of the Poor Are Still with Us: 25 Years of Working to Empower the Poor*. Washington, D.C.: United States Catholic Conference, 1995.

———. *Economic Justice for All*. Washington, D.C.: United States Catholic Conference, 1986.

———. *Renewing the Earth: An Invitation to Reflection and Action on Environment in Light of Catholic Social Teaching*. Washington, D.C.: United States Catholic Conference, 1991.

———. *Sharing Catholic Social Teaching: Challenges and Directions*. Washington, D.C.: United States Catholic Conference, 1998.

United States Catholic Conference. *Putting Children and Families First: A Challenge for Our Church, Nation, and World*. Washington, D.C.: United States Catholic Conference Office for Publishing and Promotion Services, 1992.

United States Catholic Conference Administrative Board. *Relieving Third World Debt: A Call for Co-Responsibility, Justice, and Solidarity*. Washington, D.C.: United States Catholic Conference, 1989.

Music

Brown, Monica. *A Remembering Heart*. San Jose: Resource Publications, Inc., 1992.

Smith, Julie and Tim. *A Eucharistic People*. San Jose: Resource Publications, Inc., 1993.